PAINTING
ON FABRIC

Tharina Odendaal and Anika Pretorius

ACKNOWLEDGEMENTS

THANKS FROM THARINA

I would like to thank the following people:

My parents for the opportunities and all the years of support and motivation; my husband Ernst and children Driaan and Marthinus for their patience; my friends for their interest and encouragement; my students for their never-ending questions; my two colleagues, Leoni and Diana, for their help and support; Susan Langeveldt for her computer graphics; and Anika, without whom this book would never have seen the light.

THANKS FROM ANIKA

I would like to thank:

Tharina for the hours and hours of work she put into the most beautiful paintings on fabric, which were my inspiration for this book; my husband Casper who supported me whenever I got a new idea, dreamt with me and helped me to bring it into being; my children Hannes, Herman and Jané who helped to formulate plans, for their help, patience and support; my parents and relatives who have been an inspiration to me all my life, because they all like to work and accept new challenges; Nellie Skozana without whose help in the home I would only have been able to dream and not achieve anything in practice; Leoni and Diana for helping Tharina with the examples, their moral support and encouragement; Susan Langeveldt for her computer graphics; Struik Publishers who were prepared to accept our idea and bring it to fruition; and last but not least, everyone at Struik Publishers, particularly Joy Clack the editor, who helped to create this lovely book from the manuscript – we know you worked just as hard as we did.

The authors and publishers also wish to thank the following outlets for their kind assistance and the loan of the fabric paints and props for the photography: Banks, Bric-a-Brac Lane, Plush Bazaar, Pomegranate and Zieper's Fabrics.

Struik Publishers (Pty) Ltd
(a member of Struik New Holland Publishing (Pty) Ltd)
Cornelis Struik House
80 McKenzie Street
Cape Town
8001

Reg. No.: 1954/000965/07

First published in 2000

10 9 8 7 6 5 4 3 2 1

Publishing Manager: Linda de Villiers
Editor: Joy Clack
Concept designer: Petal Palmer
Designer: Beverley Dodd
Photographer: Craig Fraser
Stylist: Sonya Nel

Reproduction by Hirt & Carter Cape (Pty) Ltd
Printed and bound by SNP Printing Pte Ltd, Singapore

ISBN 1 86872 525 1

contents

PREFACE

One day about nine years ago I went to fetch my daughter from nursery school. Instead of child art on the lines on which the works of art were usually hung out to dry, I was greeted that day by a rainbow of tablecloths on display. These were done by Tharina, one of the mothers who had recently arrived in Pretoria from Gonubie. They were so beautiful that to this day I can remember how some of those tablecloths looked. Some had guinea-fowl, others had shells printed on the fabric with blue paint and then finished in the loveliest colours by using the scraping technique.

Tharina and I met soon afterwards and discovered that we had known each other as toddlers. We both attended the same primary school and were also both past pupils of the Afrikaans Girls' High School in Pretoria. We became friends and in the course of time began to work together. I helped her to make quilted tea cosies and place mats, aprons and similar articles, since she was unable to cope with both sewing and painting. Later I cut out skirts which Tharina then painted and which we sold with matching T-shirts, also painted by her.

Gradually Tharina moved away from screen printing and increasingly began to paint on the fabric, and the more I saw her work, the more I realised that she was in a class of her own. I kept on telling her to write a book, but her answer was always the same – there was no time and she would much rather paint. In the meantime she also began giving classes at her home and she could hardly keep up. Her students came from all over, and once they started, they kept on with the classes, firstly because they learned so much and enjoyed their painting and secondly because it was such fun to be with Tharina in her studio.

About a year ago I heard that there was an urgent need for a book about fabric painting. When I told Tharina about it, we decided to grab this wonderful opportunity and enjoy every minute of it. Neither of us could work full-time on the book. Tharina was still working full-time painting to order and giving classes, and I was doing freelance editing for an educational publisher and giving afternoon classes in maths. Towards the end I often worked at her house on her husband's computer while she told me what to write while she was painting.

Only at the end of the project, when all the examples were numbered and unpacked, did we really see how hard we had worked. All the hard work, however, proved to be a wonderful experience and it is our wish that whoever handles this book and uses it will enjoy it, learn a great deal and get the inspiration to paint something themself.

ANIKA PRETORIUS

INTRODUCTION

So many opportunites have come my way to prepare me for the delightful work I am doing – so delightful that every day is the best day of my life.

I was privileged to obtain a degree in Fine Art at the University of Pretoria, with painting as a major. After that I had wonderful work opportunities and also had time to do postgraduate studies in museology and to obtain a Higher Teaching Diploma. Each work opportunity spotlighted different aspects of art and also fabric printing for me – first at the SABC as décor designer, then at Melrose House (a Victorian home museum) as curator, and then as a designer at a firm which does screen printing. In between I gave classes in painting, woodcarving and screen printing. Since 1985 I began to concentrate full-time on fabric printing. This has systematically changed into fabric painting. During the last few years I started giving classes again and increasingly realised how great the interest is in this form of handwork. I also became aware of all the questions asked by every student or interested party.

Since I derive so much pleasure from my profession, I felt that I would like to share my experience with others. I thought a lot about a title for the book and eventually decided on *Painting on Fabric*. There are many different techniques for making an artwork on fabric. In this book only one technique is discussed, namely the technique of painting on fabric. The other techniques which I touch on in passing, I usually use in combination with the painting technique, or to complement the painting. I would like, however, to emphasize that no one technique is better or more correct than another. Each one is only one of many that can be used.

I would also like to emphasize that this book will be of particular use to beginners. I start with very simple designs and I believe that if the basic designs are studied well and mastered they will provide a firm foundation so that any other design can be tackled.

Step-by-step instructions are provided for making articles of painted fabric. The methods and patterns provided were adapted over time to suit each individual painted article and to eliminate any unnecessary fuss.

May every reader make a great success of every project undertaken. Who knows, you may even discover a talent in yourself that you never even suspected you had before.

THARINA ODENDAAL

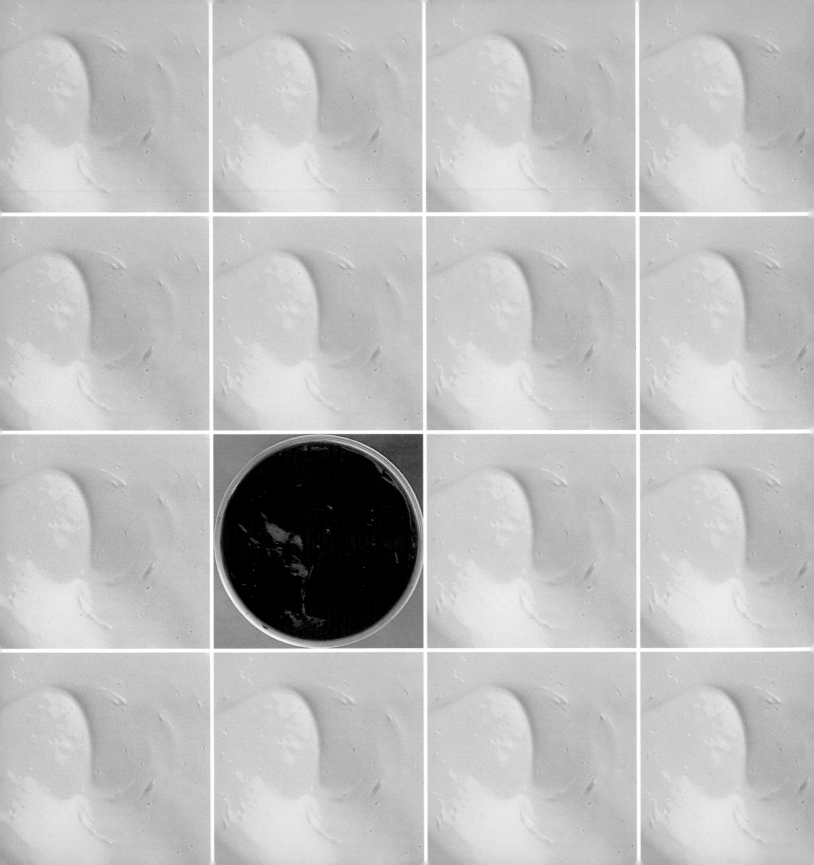

Requirements & techniques

Good planning and preparation are of the utmost importance when any project is tackled – painting on fabric is no exception. You not only have to decide on a design and colour scheme, but you must keep in mind where and how the end product is going to be used. Make a list of all the requirements and buy them in advance so that you can paint without interruption. Knowledge of a few basic techniques will also help ensure that everything runs smoothly and successfully.

GENERAL REQUIREMENTS

It is not at all expensive to take up this hobby. All that is really necessary is fabric, a few different colours of fabric paint, a couple of brushes and a flat surface on which to work. See to it that you have an apron or a set of clothes you don't mind messing on. No matter how carefully you work you always get a smudge of paint on your hands, arms or clothes. However, to make things easier, a few guidelines for items you may wish to purchase have been provided below.

BRUSHES

Ordinary pig bristle brushes work well on fabric. The harder and stiffer the brushes, the better. Buy no. 2, 5 and 10 brushes to start off with. It's also useful to have at least one very fine brush for fine detail.

IF YOU PREFER STIFFER BRUSHES, YOU CAN CUT THE BRISTLES A LITTLE SHORTER AND THIN THEM OUT TO THE BOTTOM BY SHAVING THEM LIGHTLY WITH A BLADE.

SCRAPERS

Scrapers are used to paint large plain areas or broad borders, as well as for the technique where a whole piece of fabric is covered in random blocks of different colours. This technique is called the scraping technique (see page 27).

Scrapers can be bought at a hardware shop. They are usually used to apply tile adhesive and are smooth on one side and serrated on the other. If you can't get hold of scrapers, you can cut up pieces of hard cardboard into different widths, or you could even use old credit cards.

X-RAY FILMS

Old X-ray films are very useful when you are painting. They can be used as a guide when painting borders or to make pattern templates. Clean them, if necessary, by soaking the films in a strong solution of bleach and then scrubbing them with a nailbrush.

SPONGES

Sponge blocks are used to smooth out and finish scraped borders or the background. It is easiest to use the same kind of sponges as those used in the kitchen, or sponges that are used as packaging material.

Sheets of sponge about 1 cm (⅜ in) thick are also used to cover the whole work surface. They absorb all excess paint and protect the work surface.

LIGHT-TABLE

A light-table is very useful when drawing designs. Different sizes are available, but it is better to get the largest size you can afford because it is much easier to plan the designs on a large one than on a small one.

When you start painting on fabric, you will need the following equipment to enable you to make a success of your projects: a suitable work surface covered with sponge, a selection of brushes, a scraper, a sponge, permanent markers, X-ray films, masking tape, some fabric and a light-table to trace your designs.

If you can't get hold of a light-table at all, you can improvise. Place a large, rectangular piece of thick, clear glass with each of its short sides on the edge of a table or dresser, then place a light under the glass. This works very well, but do be careful of electric shock or glass that is too thin as it could break. The glass could also crack if the light is too near and the glass becomes too hot.

DRAWING REQUIREMENTS

Keep the following items near your work table or working surface: pencils; erasers; a long, undamaged ruler (measured in centimetres); a tape measure; differently coloured pens with indelible ink; paper for notes and designs; cellophane paper on which to draw the designs and in which to pack your products; masking tape, and an outliner (a plastic squeeze bottle containing fabric paint).

A TABLE TENNIS TABLE ON TRESTLES IN YOUR GARAGE WORKS VERY WELL AS A WORK SURFACE. IT'S NOT ONLY NICE AND WIDE, BUT SHOULD ANY WATER SPILL ON IT, IT'S NOT THE SAME TRAGEDY AS WHEN IT MESSES ON YOUR EXPENSIVE DINING ROOM TABLE.

PREPARATION OF WORK SURFACE AND TOOLS

Any flat surface is suitable for working on. For example, a large table is very useful for painting large articles such as tablecloths, while a flat piece of wood or a tray on your lap or on a table is ideal for painting small items such as place mats or serviettes. A large drawing board, or even an easel with a large board covered with sponge, on which the fabric can hang and be fastened with big paper clips, works very well for painting wall hangings, pictures or blinds. But take care that the table is neither too high nor too low when you are working, or you could easily get a sore back if you paint for a long time.

Always cover any surface you intend working on with a layer of sponge about 1 cm (⅜ in) thick. The sponge ensures that the fabric does not move around while you are painting and absorbs superfluous paint which could otherwise penetrate the surface. It also prevents the back of the fabric from being smeared with paint.

Clear away all unnecessary items from the work table and thoroughly clean the surface. Check that there is no wet paint from a previous project on the table's surface – wet paint can spoil both the new project and your clothes. It also happens that you get paint on your arm or hand and unknowingly dirty everything in this way.

See to it that there are always enough clean brushes and clean containers for the paint, as well as a jar of clean water.

THE FABRIC

When you paint on fabric, your choice of fabric is vital. The eventual choice usually depends on what you have in mind for the end product. The purpose of the article as well as the effect you wish to create both play a role.

CHOICE OF FABRIC

The composition and texture of the fabric dictate to a degree how paint is going to react to it, so a careful choice is necessary.

Tablecloth fabric is suitable for tablecloths, tea cosies, blinds and wall hangings. Sheeting on the other hand is better for curtains, sheets and pillowcases. Unbleached linen works well for wall hangings, pictures and place mats, and white denim is suitable for single-layer place mats and bags.

Paint reacts differently on different kinds of fabric. On some fabrics it is difficult to achieve a smooth effect, but it could also be just the right thing to show up an interesting texture or brush marks. Other fabrics also allow the paint to spread a further 2.5 cm (1 in) from where it was brushed on, which results in a specific effect. All the different fabrics are not always obtainable everywhere, so buy a remnant and first test it to see if it gives the desired effect.

Check the fabric you intend using before you start painting. It should preferably be woven from natural fibres such as cotton, silk, linen or viscose. However, most of the fabrics that look like cotton are cotton and polyester blends. The difficulty with these fabrics is that the paint washes out more quickly and the design becomes fainter after each wash. This can be partially prevented by not washing the painted fabric too soon after painting, and by using one of the heat treatments to fix the paint (see page 29).

Pure cotton always works very well, although it creases badly and is not always available. Cotton knit fabric also works well, except that it absorbs paint with greater difficulty and it is harder to apply paint to it than to woven fabric. You can make gorgeous, exclusive T-shirts by buying plain cotton T-shirts at chain stores and painting designs on them.

To test whether fabric is made of pure cotton or is a blend, burn a little fragment of it with a match. If it is cotton, it will burn slowly to form a fine ash. If it contains polyester, it will burn quickly and stick together to resemble black, melted plastic.

PREPARATION OF FABRIC

When you buy fabric, make provision for the fact that fabrics made of natural fibres can shrink when washed. So buy about 10 per cent more fabric than you need.

Thoroughly wash all fabrics made of natural fibre, such as unbleached linen, pure cotton and linen, with soap in the washing machine at maximum temperature. This process is necessary to remove all starch and other impurities and to shrink the fabric before using. Hang it outside until almost dry and then iron it thoroughly with a very hot iron.

Keep the fabric away from any paint until the design has been drawn on it. Remember, dirt on the fabric cannot be disguised by paint and this could ruin a lovely article. Also cut the fabric square before you draw a design on it. You cannot remedy a skew piece of fabric with a design on it by pulling or cutting it correctly later on.

> MAKE SURE YOUR FABRIC CAN BE TORN TO THE REQUIRED SIZE. ALTERNATIVELY, PULL A THREAD BEFORE CUTTING IT TO SIZE.

BUYING & MIXING PAINT

When you buy paint, it is important to make sure that it is meant for use on textiles. The containers ought to be marked 'fabric paint/textile paint'. If you are not sure whether the paint is suitable, rather leave it and go to another dealer. A lot of time and work goes into every article and if you do not use the right paint the article will not be able to be washed or cleaned later on.

It is very easy to work with fabric paint. The paint is water-soluble, odourless and non-toxic. The paint is usually composed of two components, namely a white emulsion or transparent base (extender), which looks like joiner's glue, and a pigment which looks like coloured ink. You can buy the paint ready-mixed, or you can buy the emulsion and pigment separately and mix them yourself. If you are making articles for sale, or you are making large articles, the latter is by far the cheaper option. Some people refer to the paint as ink, but that is confusing as the ready-mixed paint looks more like a paste than ink.

There are different kinds of fabric paint, so be quite sure that you buy the paint you really want. The different kinds are:

Transparent colours (Coloured paint)
Most of the examples in this book were painted with this paint. The different colours can be painted over each other to create new colours.

Partly transparent paint (Semi-opaque paint)
The colours of these paints are precisely what the name says they are – partly transparent.

Non-transparent paint (Opaque paint)
An example of this is opaque white. All paints can be covered with this paint.

Metal colours (Metallic paint)
A touch of gold, silver or bronze can finish off an article very attractively. It looks lovely when some of the outlines of a design are retraced in gold, silver or bronze. In this book gold powder mixed with metallic medium has been used. But use these paints sparingly because they are very expensive.

Pearl colours (Pearly paint)
These paints have a pearly sheen to them when used, and are very effective for decorative work.

Puff paint
This is paint that puffs up and feels almost like plastic. The puff effect is activated by heat.

Transparent base (Cut Clear or Extender)
This product is used as a base for mixing in colour pigments. It is also added to ready-mixed colours to lighten them.

It is a good idea, when starting, to buy a couple of basic ready-mixed transparent colours and some transparent base with which to lighten the colours. Experiment with mixing colours and remember to write down what you did to get a certain colour.

When you mix light colours, it's always better to put the transparent base in the bowl first, and then add a little bit of colour at a time to get the required colour, rather than doing it the other way around.

Start off with a small selection of basic colours and add to your collection as you gain more experience

BASIC COLOURS

To start with, buy the following four basic colours:

- ❖ **Blue:** navy
- ❖ **Yellow:** primrose yellow
- ❖ **Magenta:** magenta
  (not the same as the ready-mixed maroon)
- ❖ **Red:** brilliant red

A variety of colours can be mixed from the four basic colours and transparent base:

- ❖ **Orange:** yellow + red
- ❖ **Apricot:** yellow + red + magenta + base
- ❖ **Peach:** yellow + magenta + base
- ❖ **Brown:** yellow + red + magenta + blue
- ❖ **Toffee:** brown + yellow + base
- ❖ **Mustard:** brown + a lot of yellow + base
- ❖ **Terracotta:** yellow + quite a lot of magenta
- ❖ **Cherry:** yellow + a lot of magenta
- ❖ **Yellow-green:** a lot of yellow + blue
- ❖ **Olive green:** blue + yellow
- ❖ **Blue-green:** a lot of blue + yellow
- ❖ **Black:** yellow + red + blue + magenta
- ❖ **Jacaranda blue:** blue + a little magenta + base
- ❖ **Purple:** blue + magenta
- ❖ **Grape purple:** magenta + a little blue
- ❖ **Pink-purple:** a little magenta + a dash of blue + base

> KEEP A NOTEBOOK IN WHICH TO JOT
> DOWN NOTES ON EVERY PROJECT, RIGHT
> FROM THE START. INDICATE WHAT FABRIC YOU
> BOUGHT AND HOW MUCH OF IT, HOW YOU
> MIXED THE PAINT AND ANY OTHER INFORMATION.
> YOU ALWAYS NEED THIS INFORMATION LATER
> AND, BELIEVE ME, IT'S NO USE TRYING TO
> RELY ON MEMORY.

ADDITIONAL COLOURS

Gradually buy at least the following colours:

- **Blue:** royal blue
- **Brown:** golden brown
- **Yellow:** golden yellow (more orange than primrose yellow)
- **Green:** bright green, emerald green
- **Gold:** metallic gold
- **Purple:** violet
- **Turquoise:** turquoise
- **Black:** black
- **White:** opaque white

The loveliest sea greens can be mixed from combinations of turquoise, emerald green and navy. Since blue and green give an olive green, the bright green and emerald green are necessary to provide another series of greens.

ALL COLOURS CAN BE MADE LIGHTER
BY ADDING BASE (EXTENDER).

The following colours were all mixed with the four basic colours, the extra 16 colours and base:

- **Yellow-green**
- **Apple green**
- **Dark green**
- **Bottle green**
- **Peacock blue**
- **Purple-blue**

If you use a lot of brown and black paint in your work, it is advisable to buy these colours ready-mixed.

Use your paint sparingly and never mix too much. If the paint is not used within a short space of time, the colours will become dull and dirty and the paint will get a grainy texture, which doesn't look good on the fabric as it starts to dry out. If, however, you are tackling a large project which you can't complete in one day, for instance curtains, it is better to mix a good deal of paint in advance since it is very difficult to get the exact colours again.

Mix the paint in plastic containers with lids, such as ice cream containers, and pour out just enough for your painting into a polystyrene dish.

You must **never** mix the paint directly on the fabric. Also make sure that the colour is perfectly blended before you begin to paint with it, otherwise you could end up with streaks of unblended colours.

DESIGNS

Everything in nature is three-dimensional, so if you want to paint designs that others will recognize, you need to create a three-dimensional illusion. To be able to create this illusion in paint, the most important skill to acquire is the ability 'to see'. This process of learning 'to see' is a wonderful experience. Suddenly you see detail and miracles in nature that you were never aware of before.

Reality is the best teacher. If you want to paint leaves, flowers or fruit, for instance, you first have to look very carefully at real leaves, flowers and fruit. Look at the different shapes and colours. Take note of the difference in colour and texture between the top and bottom of a leaf, or of the skins of different fruits. Draw different leaves, flowers and fruits. For example, take a real orange, cut it in half, look at the segments and observe how they look when the light falls on them from different angles and where the shadows fall each time. Once you know how to draw the object, you'll be able to paint it more easily.

CHOICE OF DESIGN

Never start painting before you have planned what you want to do. Depending on the size of the design, you should plan the shape and distribution of colour. Don't portray all the objects in the design directly from the front, but try to depict them from different angles.

Also pay attention to differences in texture. Different textures can make a design much more interesting, and can also create a certain atmosphere or feeling within a design.

Lighting plays a very important role in design. Remember, light usually comes from one side. If the light comes directly from the front, the object will look flat. It therefore looks much better if the light falls from one side and there are shadows which give depth to the design.

The above examples of pencil drawings can be used as a base for developing more advanced designs.

ENLARGING AND REDUCING DESIGNS

Most of the designs used for painting on fabric, just like the ones included in this book, are not the right size and usually need to be enlarged. The easiest way of enlarging designs is by using a photostat machine. Unfortunately it's not always possible to get the right size at once on an ordinary machine and the design sometimes has to be repeatedly enlarged until it's the right size. Some of the larger towns and cities have facilities available to get any desired size, but it is quite costly.

An alternative is to draw a grid over the design. This means drawing equal sized blocks, say 1 x 1 cm (⅜ x ⅜ in), over the whole design. To enlarge the design, you draw an equal number of blocks, say 2 x 2 cm (¾ x ¾ in) or 10 x 10 cm (4 x 4 in) on another, larger piece of paper. The design is then redrawn, block by block, from the smaller to the larger blocks. By using 2 cm (¾ in) blocks you will double the size of the design, and by using 10 cm (4 in) blocks you will make it 10 times larger.

Use a grid with blocks to enlarge the design.

DON'T SUMMARILY DECIDE THAT YOU CAN'T PAINT ON FABRIC IF YOU HAVE A HARD TIME DESIGNING SOMETHING ON YOUR OWN. FEEL FREE TO USE THE DESIGNS IN THIS BOOK, AND ALSO DESIGNS AVAILABLE COMMERCIALLY.

If you are going to use a single design, for example when you are going to paint lemons on a tablecloth, it is necessary to plan the composition beforehand. In other words, decide how and where the lemons are going to be arranged on the tablecloth. Enlarge the lemon just once to the desired size and then draw the same lemon in different positions on the tablecloth.

IT IS IMPORTANT TO ORGANIZE YOUR DESIGNS RIGHT FROM THE START. GOOD DESIGNS ARE YOUR GREATEST ASSET AND IF YOU DON'T LOOK AFTER THEM THEY DISAPPEAR. FILE ALL IDEAS AND PICTURES ACCORDING TO SUBJECT. FILE ALL DESIGNS THAT NEED TO BE ENLARGED IN ANOTHER FILE. ALL DESIGNS THAT ARE READY TO USE AND ARE ALREADY DRAWN IN INK ON PAPER OR CELLOPHANE, CAN BE ROLLED UP NEATLY OR STORED IN A PORTFOLIO. IT'S ALSO A GOOD IDEA TO NUMBER ALL THESE DESIGNS AND KEEP A LIST OF THEM IN YOUR NOTEBOOK. REMEMBER TO MAKE A NOTE OF IT IF YOU LEND A DESIGN TO ANYONE.

COMBINING BASIC DESIGNS

Many of the designs used in this book are combinations of a few basic designs. When such a design is assembled, you need to know where and how the design is going to be used.

Make a rough sketch planning which designs you want to use and how you want to arrange them on the article.

When a new design is being assembled from individual designs, the scale of the designs must be the same. You can't draw a strawberry and a lemon the same size – their size should be in proportion to each other. Once the individual designs have been enlarged to the required size, trace them onto cellophane or transparent paper. Play around with the different designs and then trace the fully assembled design onto paper.

For the central design of a tablecloth, for instance, start at the middle of the cloth. Then arrange the designs in the corners, and then in the spaces in between.

In a border pattern, work horizontally from the middle of the design towards the outside. Take care that the distances between individual designs are the same on both sides so that the design is symmetrical.

If you want to repeat a design four times on your fabric, it is useful to fold the fabric in half and in half again. Iron lightly so that when the fabric is unfolded, you will clearly see four equal squares, enabling the designs to be positioned more easily.

> IT WORKS BEST TO TRACE THE WHOLE DESIGN ON PAPER AND THEN TRACE FROM THE PAPER ONTO THE FABRIC. YOU CAN GET CHEAP ROLLS OF CLEAN NEWSPAPER FROM ALL NEWSPAPER PRINTERS. REMEMBER THAT IT IS VERY DIFFICULT TO PAINT OUT LINES THAT HAVE BEEN INCORRECTLY DRAWN ON FABRIC, OR EVEN TO ERASE PENCIL LINES.

APPLYING DESIGNS TO FABRIC

When the design is the desired size, the lines must be clearly drawn in black permanent ink onto strong plastic, cellophane or paper. The lines must be very clear as they have to show up through the fabric.

The ideal way of transferring the design onto the fabric is to use a light-table (see page 8), as the pattern shows up very well on it. If you don't have access to a light-table and can't improvise one, there are a few other ways to trace the pattern onto the fabric:

❖ Place the pattern, which has been drawn on white paper, under the fabric and trace it with a pencil, fabric marker or directly with an outliner (plastic squeeze bottle). If the pattern is drawn very clearly it works very well on white or any other light-coloured fabric. It is preferable not to use a pencil on the fabric since pencil marks can't easily be removed from fabric should you make a mistake.

❖ Dressmaker's carbon-paper can be placed face-down on top of the fabric and under the pattern. The pattern can then be traced, even with an empty ballpoint pen, since the carbon comes off on the fabric when pressed. This method is usually used on dark-coloured fabrics which are not transparent.

❖ If a small design is to be traced onto a small piece of fabric and you can't make another plan, you can use natural light to trace the design onto the fabric. Place the paper pattern on a clear glass windowpane with the fabric on top, then trace the design.

> A BORDER PATTERN ON A TABLECLOTH CAN BE REPEATED ON A TEA SHOWER OR TEA COSY TO MAKE A MATCHING SET.

These examples of border designs have been composed from some of the basic designs at the back of the book.

COLOUR USAGE

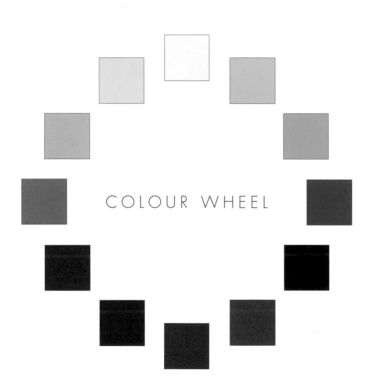

COLOUR WHEEL

Study this colour wheel to get a feeling for colour.

CHOOSING COLOURS FOR A DESIGN

Choosing the right colours is almost as important as the design itself. If you use a poor colour scheme even a good design will not show up well, and can even be ruined by it. The reverse can also happen when a very simple design looks beautiful, just because the colours have been cleverly chosen.

Make time to play with colours and experiment. The time you spend on this is an investment and will eventually save you a lot of heartache. Paint colours next to each other on sample bits of fabric and see how they 'react' to one another. Just remember that colours become lighter as they dry and that they react differently on different fabrics. The more you play, the more you'll get a feeling for colour. It is also important to remember that this is exactly the way to develop your own style, which will be quite different to anybody else's. Make strips with examples of colours for your notebook and remember to write down exactly what you did to get a specific colour.

The most gorgeous colour combinations are usually achieved by using together colours on the opposite sides of the colour wheel. Just think of dark blue with yellow, lime green with purple, and green with orange.

If you are in doubt about a colour, look at nature. Just look around you in the garden at the colours of flowers, leaves and grass or at the colours of sea-plants and animals in a rock pool near the shore. Brightly coloured flowers are often surrounded by bright green leaves, while delicate blue flowers generally have fewer leaves that are a duller shade of green. Lemons, which are a bright, strong yellow, show up best against the hard, strong and bright green leaves of a lemon tree. Also think about the different earthy colours seen in a dry area or desert.

When you look at a flower or leaf, you will never see just one shade of a colour. There are always shadows and variations. When you can see this and can reflect it in your work, you'll have begun to paint creatively. This is why the book is called *Painting on Fabric*, because you are, in a sense, producing a work of art.

THE OUTLINES OF A DESIGN

Different colours can be used to draw the outlines of the design on the fabric. Sometimes even two colours are used for outlines in one design. Each colour, however, creates a different effect, as you can see from the examples below.

You can use different media for the outlines. Only three have been used in this book, namely a pencil, fabric marker and outliners filled with different colours of paint. The pens and bottles of paint are readily available at hobby and art shops.

In the first example the pattern is traced onto the fabric with a very light pencil (the design can also be painted directly onto the fabric with a brush). This method is usually used to create a very natural effect, for instance when a wall painting is being made. The leaves at the back of a design are usually painted in this manner so that it looks as though they are far away.

In the following two examples the outlines are drawn with different coloured paints in bottles. The difference in effect is very clear and the different colours can create a completely new atmosphere within the design.

Outlines, which eventually are touched up with gold, silver or bronze paint, also look very fetching. This can turn a simple article into something very professional and special.

> BUY EMPTY PLASTIC SQUEEZE BOTTLES WITH A NOZZLE AND CAP AND FILL THEM WITH READY-MADE PAINT. THIS IS MUCH CHEAPER AND YOU CAN USE UNUSUAL COLOURS THAT YOU MIX YOURSELF.

Outlines create different effects: there is no outline on the first example, while the second and third examples are outlined in different colours.

PAINTING TECHNIQUES

There are many different ways of applying paint. No single one of them is a right, better or wrong method. Each person in the end chooses a technique or develops an individual technique which suits his or her personality and style.

When you create a work of art you need to add a third dimension of depth. You achieve this by varying the different shades of colour. It is not so easy to reproduce this variation, and therefore it is necessary to look at real flowers, leaves, fruit and shells before you start painting. When you do this you will suddenly see a lot of detail you were not aware of before, and will slowly but surely begin to develop a feeling for depth and colour. I'd also like to predict that from now on you will always look at a flower or a blade of grass with new eyes.

The techniques used and discussed in this book have taken years to develop to give the desired results. Try these techniques and make your own experiments until you find something you like and with which you achieve the effects you seek. No two people will have or should have an identical product, and that is exactly what makes this form of art so rewarding.

THERE ARE NO RULES! ANY TECHNIQUE IS PERMISSIBLE, AS LONG AS YOU FIND IT ATTRACTIVE AND YOU ENJOY PAINTING.

By using different shades of colour you can create depth and a more natural, three-dimensional effect in the design.

PAINTING TECHNIQUE

Requirements
- Any fabric of natural fibre
- A pen for the outlines of the design
- White pig bristle brushes: nos 2, 4 and 6 for small designs; 6 and 10 for large designs
- Paint

1 Leave highlight areas open on the fabric so that the natural white of the fabric is retained and so that it need not be painted in white opaque paint later on. The natural white of the fabric looks much better and more natural.

2 Paint small areas with a small brush and larger areas with a broader brush.

3 First paint the lightest colours since colours can only be made darker and not lighter. (In particular cases lighter colours can be painted over dark colours, but then opaque paint, which is not transparent, must be used.) The light colour is then painted over with a darker colour.

4 Paint the lightest colours over a larger area than they are meant to cover. This will help the darker colours blend in and ensures that there is no boundary between the colours.

5 Always try to complete a whole section or object in one sitting, while it is still wet. This will make sure that the colours blend in better.

6 Remember, wet paint is always darker than dry paint. If you are in doubt about a colour, first test it on a remnant of the same fabric and let it dry completely.

PERSPECTIVE

When you paint a design, it usually has more than one object. The objects do not all lie next to each other, but some are to the front and others towards the back. If you paint them all the same colour, you are going to get a very flat picture. To achieve depth you need to paint the objects in such a way that you can immediately see that one lies in front of the other.

In the example above, therefore, you need to create the illusion that one pear is hanging in front of the other on the tree. From the sketch you can clearly see that the pear on the right is hanging in front because the pear on the left is not drawn completely. You must, however, also indicate by colour that the one pear is hanging in front of the other.

Work in the same way as when any other pear is painted (see pages 42–43). Pay attention, however, to the following:

❖ Make the highlights of the pear in front larger than those on the pear at the back.
❖ Use darker colours for the pear at the back than you use for the pear in front.
❖ Paint the darkest parts of the pear at the back on the right-hand side behind the pear in front.

BACKGROUND

There are many ways and techniques to paint the background. In this book we discuss three. The first technique is for an even, plain background. Using the second technique the background is painted three-dimensionally, and in the third the background is scraped in. These techniques are used in all the examples since they are well suited to the painting technique used.

Even, plain background

This technique is mostly used on small areas, such as small tablecloths, place mats and tea cosies, but if the background is painted in neatly and evenly, it can also look very good on larger articles. But do pay attention to the sort of fabric you use. Some fabrics work better than others and usually look nicer because the end product has a smoother and softer texture. Before you begin to tackle a whole project, do a test on a remnant of the same fabric and leave it to dry out well in order to see the final result.

Requirements
- Scrapers of different widths
- Brushes of different thicknesses
- Old X-ray films
- Masking tape of different widths
- Sponge blocks
- Paint

1 When a background is painted using this technique, you must have enough time to finish the whole background in one sitting. If you were to stop, it would leave a definite mark which would spoil the whole article.

2 Make sure that you have enough paint to cover the whole background. Even if you do everything in exactly the same way, the colour will never be exactly the same, and in such a large area it will definitely show up.

3 Choose the colour for the background very carefully, especially if you are thinking of making a border in another colour. To ensure that the colours do not flow into each other, you can create a dividing line by sticking down a strip of masking tape. Take care that the masking tape adheres very well, otherwise the paint will flow under it if it is not pressed down properly. This is not such a big problem if you are using two colours that blend well, but when you are using colours such as purple and yellow, and they mix, you get an ugly brown that usually does not suit the rest of the colours.

4 Well-scrubbed X-ray films can also be used to create straight boundaries between colours.

5 Make sure that the paint is mixed very well. If the paint is not well mixed, the uneven colour will show up very clearly when the scraper is pulled over it.

The plain royal blue background is a good contrast to the bright yellow sunflowers.

6 Start painting with a brush those areas where the scraper is not going to be used, for example the area between leaves or the borders of the design.

7 Use the scrapers to scrape the large open spaces. Stop every few minutes and rub hard over the painted surface with the sponge so that the paint is as even and smooth as it can be.

8 It is sometimes necessary to apply two coats of paint to the whole area. Make sure, however, that you apply the same amount of paint over the whole area, otherwise the background will be streaky and full of marks when the paint dries.

Three-dimensional background

This technique is used to emphasize the three-dimensional design in the foreground.

Requirements
- Brushes of different thicknesses
- Paint

1 When painting flowers, you need to create the impression that the flowers are part of a bunch in nature or a garden. The distance of the leaves that are farthest away is suggested by the absence of outlining, using only brushwork. The farther to the back, the less detail is portrayed. The leaves thus become less realistic and the veins on the leaves more and more dull.

2 To create the illusion that there are many more flowers in the background, you can apply a lighter colour to the background than that which is used in the flowers in the foreground.

3 To portray the sky, use very pale blues, which can sometimes even be painted over the leaves at the back. Always try to finish painting the sky areas in one sitting to ensure a gentle and misty effect. If you allow the paint to dry and start painting again later, clear watermarks will be visible on the fabric.

4 In some cases, however, you will need to let the paint dry completely to prevent the colours from spreading. You would need to do this, for example, when painting leaves of different colours where you don't want the different shades of green to run into each other.

Watery paint can be sprinkled over the background to emphasize the 3-D effect.

5 You can also achieve interesting effects by painting light, misty colours randomly and letting them dry. Combinations of, for instance, pale turquoise, blue and yellow look marvellous. Allow the paint to dry and then dilute a little contrasting colour of paint with water until it almost looks like coloured water. Drop or splash drops of this paint over the paint dried earlier. This method can be used for the backs of place mats, pillows or bags.

Scraped background

The scraping technique is very quick, easy and effective in any combination of colours. It works very well for large areas like blinds and curtains.

The scraping technique effect is clearly depicted in this example.

Requirements

- Scrapers of different widths
- Paint

1 Choose and mix all the paint needed for the project before you begin painting. Remember, too, to mix enough paint to complete the whole project.

2 Place the different coloured paints in separate containers that are wider than the scrapers.

3 Use the lightest colour or the colour that you want to display the most, first.

4 Press the scraper into the paint at a slant of about 30 degrees so that there is more paint on one side of the scraper than on the other.

5 Pull the scraper over the fabric at the same angle you pulled it through the paint. You can pull it in any direction and over any distance. The marks may be solid or broken. If the marks are uneven, they form very interesting patterns and designs over which other colours may be scraped later on.

6 First scrape over the whole area with one colour before you work with a second or third colour. This ensures that the colours will be evenly spread and that the fabric will not be darker on one side than on the other, unless that is the way you planned it.

7 With this technique, the colours can be scraped over each other even if the bottom layer is still wet.

8 If, at the end, you feel that you see too little of a particular colour, you can scrape that colour over the other colours once again.

9 Remember that the whole area can be covered with paint or you can leave open white patches on the fabric.

A PLAIN BORDER

Many articles are finished with a plain border of 4–10 cm (1⅝–4 in) right round. In order to get this border straight and of the same width, well-scrubbed X-ray films and a scraper are usually used.

1 Decide how wide you want the border to be and add an extra 2–3 mm (¹⁄₁₆–⅛ in) which the over-locker will cut off.

2 Make a few dots to act as a guide on each side of the fabric. This should preferably be done with a purple marker which can wash out.

3 Choose the colour for the border very carefully. Strong colours like navy blue and dark greens usually work very well.

4 Press the side of the X-ray film very firmly on the inside of the fabric against the dots. Start applying the paint with a scraper. Always scrape away from the film and make sure that no paint gets in under it. The superfluous paint can be sponged off carefully and smoothed out evenly.

5 Let the border dry completely before picking up the article and folding it.

When making a double border, make sure the lighter border is completely dry before scraping the second, darker border.

HEAT TREATMENTS

When you use textile paint on fabric, the colours have to be fixed to make them colourfast. This means that some process or other has to be employed to prevent the colours from fading as a result of exposure to light or from washing out. Usually heat is used, but different kinds of paint may require different methods to bring this about. It is therefore important to read very carefully all the instructions that come with the paint and to follow them precisely.

The paints used in this book, and most of the other paints available, are fixed by heat, and the instuctions given below can normally be used as a guideline. You can use the heat of an oven, tumble-drier or iron. If, however, you want to make vast amounts of fabric colourfast, some dry-cleaners will do it for you with their big roller presses.

IRON METHOD

Colours can be fixed with an ordinary iron, but then you must make sure that the whole area is treated and that the iron is held on each section long enough. This method can be used to make finished articles colourfast. The ideal way, however, is to treat the fabric before it is processed.

1 Repeatedly iron the back of the fabric with the temperature set on hot or 'cotton'. Each painted area should be ironed for at least 3 minutes.

> USE THE TUMBLE-DRIER OR IRON METHOD FOR ARTICLES LARGER THAN 3.5 M (138 IN) IN EXTENT.

TUMBLE-DRIER METHOD

Only unprocessed fabric can be treated in this way since the padding and even the thread can melt from the heat.

1 Make sure that the painted fabric is completely dry before placing it in the tumble-drier. If the paint is not dry, it will smear and the whole article will be spoiled.

2 Place the fabric in the tumble-drier at maximum heat for 30–60 minutes.

OVEN METHOD

Only unprocessed painted fabric can be treated in this way since padding and even thread can melt from the heat. Another disadvantage of this method is that only small quantities of fabric can be treated at a time.

1 Pre-heat the oven to 140 °C (300 °F).

2 Place a thick layer of newspaper or a baking tray on the oven rack with the folded fabric on top, and place the rack in the middle of the oven. Make quite sure that the fabric does not hang over the edge of the paper or baking tray, since those parts will get singed and turn brown. Also make sure that the newspaper does not touch the sides of the oven as it could burst into flames.

3 Leave the fabric in the oven for 7 minutes. If the oven light comes on during this time, immediately lower the temperature to prevent the elements from switching on.

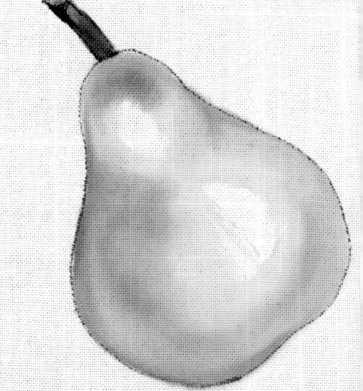

Basic designs

As with every new skill that you learn, you should start with the basics. Be careful not

to think too big in the beginning, make a mess of the project and then decide that

you can't do it. This doesn't mean that you should make an inferior article, but try to

keep the design simple and not use too many colours. Also don't be over-ambitious

and tackle a large tablecloth as a first attempt.

strawberries

Individual strawberries or an arrangement of strawberries can be used for place mats, pot holders, tea cosies, curtains, blinds and so on.

PAINT

YELLOW: primrose yellow
RED: brilliant red
MAGENTA: magenta
BLUE: navy, royal blue
GREEN: bright green, emerald green

BLENDS

Notice how the colours are applied one at a time, from lightest to darkest.

1 Using a black pen, trace the outlines of the design (see page 113) onto the fabric.

2 The strawberries in this example are half-ripe – thus the white and yellow parts at the top of each strawberry. Leave open a white highlight on each strawberry. It looks more natural and is more successful than trying to paint a highlight with opaque paint afterwards. All the colours are transparent, so colours can only be made darker and not lighter.

3 First paint with the yellow. Paint an area that is a little bigger than it will be in the end so that the other colours can easily blend into it.

4 Now paint with the red. Place the brush under the yellow and paint upwards into the yellow. In this way the red will run into the yellow and give a lovely soft effect.

5 Paint the darker areas with plain magenta. The darkest areas should be painted last with a blend of magenta and navy.

6 When all the paint is completely dry, draw in the little dots with an outliner or fabric marker. When the dots are dry, each one can be rounded off with a mixture of opaque white and yellow.

This strawberry design can be used as is for pot holders or serviettes or can be enlarged for tablecloths or blinds.

7 When the design is completely dry, paint the background royal blue. Use a sponge to even out the paint, as explained on page 24.

8 Paint the leaves in shades of green (see pages 46–47).

apples

The simple lines and colour blends of apples make them a good choice for beginners.

PAINT

YELLOW: primrose yellow
RED: brilliant red
MAGENTA: magenta
BLUE: navy, royal blue
GREEN: bright green,
  emerald green
TRANSPARENT BASE: extender
DARK BROWN: dark brown

BLENDS

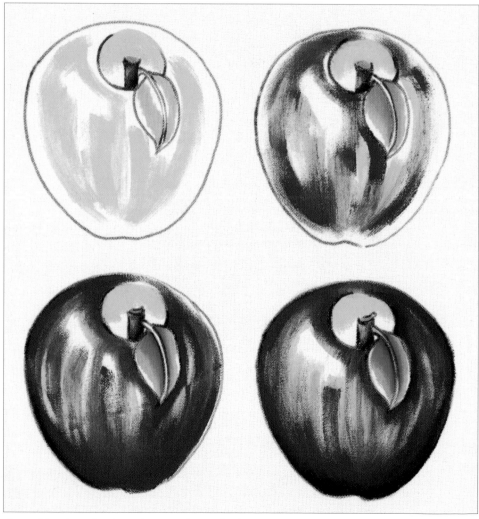

Curved brush strokes have been used to make the apples appear round.

1 Using a black pen, trace the outlines of the design (see page 114) onto the fabric.

2 Remember to leave open a white highlight on each apple. It looks much more natural and is more successful than painting in a highlight with opaque white later on.

3 Remember that the colours are transparent, so colours can only be made darker and not lighter.

4 First paint the yellow. Paint the yellow area a little larger than it will be at the end.

5 Secondly, paint the red. Paint the red from below into the yellow. The stripes made by the brush imitate the streakiness of each apple. Apply the brush strokes in the right direction so that they accentuate the shape of the apple.

6 Use magenta for the darker parts.

7 Lastly, apply the magenta and navy blend. This colour emphasizes the roundness of the apple and at the same time indicates that the apple is at rest and not floating.

8 Paint the leaves by starting with a light green on the outside of the leaves and ending with the darkest green next to the veins and also where the leaves are hidden behind the apples. Keep in mind that the veins of most leaves are normally a very light shade of green. Refer to pages 46–47 for a detailed explanation.

This design will brighten up your kitchen! Use it on pot holders, tea towels, place mats, tray cloths and tea cosies.

9 Draw and paint the stems in dark brown and ochre. Ochre is obtained by mixing magenta and yellow.

10 Use royal blue for the background. Use a sponge to even out the background (see page 24).

sunflowers

Sunflowers always look cheerful, and a few cushions, a tablecloth or curtains with sunflowers will brighten up any dull room.

PAINT

MAGENTA: magenta
YELLOW: primrose yellow,
 golden yellow
BROWN: dark brown
RED: brilliant red
BLUE: navy

BLENDS

This example of a sunflower shows how the petals are painted in stages.

1 Using a black pen, trace the outlines of the design (see page 115) onto the fabric.

2 When you paint the flowers, the dark shadowy parts of the petals are painted first, which is not usually the case. This gives better results than painting the lightest colours first. Make sure that there is enough shadow in the petals at the back to give the flower depth. Use only three shades of yellow and the white of the fabric for the petals. Mix magenta and the two shades of yellow for the darkest yellow. Use primrose yellow and golden yellow for the other two shades.

3 Use three colours for the heart of the flower (the part with the seeds) – dark brown, red-brown and ochre. Use brown and add yellow and red to get different shades. If you don't have any brown paint, you can get dark brown by mixing yellow, magenta and navy, and a reddish brown by adding more magenta. Ochre is made by mixing yellow and magenta.

Sunflowers always look cheerful and beautiful on a bright or royal blue background. The design of the sunflower at the back of the book (see page 115) was greatly enlarged and repeated three times to achieve the effect on this wall panel.

lemons

Lemons are among the loveliest and most useful designs in this book. Everyone likes these designs because they always look fresh and appealing and the colours suit any house. Paint lemons on tablecloths, curtains, pot holders and aprons and you are sure of a winner.

PAINT
YELLOW: primrose yellow
TRANSPARENT BASE: extender
GREEN: bright green
WHITE: opaque white

BLENDS

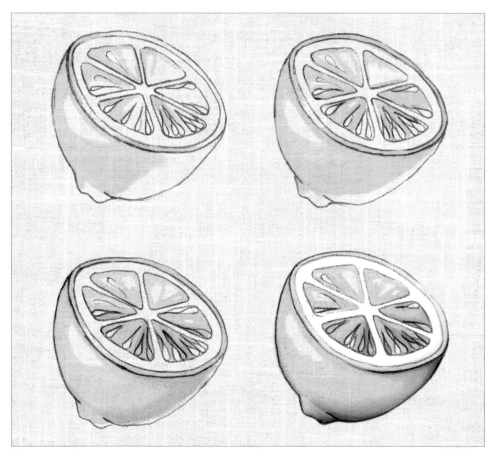

These steps illustrate how the colours are applied one at a time when painting lemons.
Notice how green is used to make the lemons appear oval.

1 Using a black pen, trace the outlines of the design (see page 116) onto the fabric.

2 Leave a white highlight open on every lemon.

3 The colours are transparent, so colours can only be made darker and not lighter.

4 Mix a little yellow paint with a lot of base and paint around the highlight.

5 Paint a darker yellow around the light yellow while the light yellow is still wet. This is done so that the colours can blend together.

6 Mix the yellow paint with a little bright green and paint it around the darker yellow on the lemon.

The design on this beautiful tablecloth appears on page 116 at the back of the book.

7 Use a yellowish green to paint in the shadows and to give depth so that the lemon appears oval.

8 When you want to paint a sliced lemon, you should cut open a real lemon and study it carefully. Have a good look at the different segments of the lemon before you begin to paint them. Use subtle shades of green in the slices to get light and shade effects. A touch of orange will also give life to the slices.

9 Paint the white part of the rind and the membranes between the segments with opaque white.

A LEMON HAS AN OVAL SHAPE, SO THE BRUSH STROKES SHOULD GO IN AN OVAL CURVE WHEN THE PAINT IS APPLIED.

oranges

When you paint a composition of fruit, oranges are indispensable and they usually complete the picture. There is no design of an orange at the back of the book because all you need to do is adapt the lemon design slightly and change the colours.

PAINT

YELLOW: golden yellow, primrose yellow
TRANSPARENT BASE: extender
MAGENTA: magenta
WHITE: opaque white

BLENDS

The curvature of the brush strokes and the highlights give the oranges a round appearance.

1 Using a black pen, trace the design onto the fabric.

2 Decide where the light is going to fall on the orange so that the white of the fabric can be left open in that area.

3 Mix a little golden yellow with transparent base to get a very pale yellow and paint around the highlights. Paint a large area with this yellow as you can always make it darker.

4 Paint undiluted golden yellow around the light yellow. This must be done while the light yellow is still wet, so that the colours blend into each other.

5 Mix golden yellow with a little magenta and paint it around the golden yellow on the orange.

6 Use a dark, reddish orange to paint in the shadows and to give more depth so that the orange appears round.

Brighten up the breakfast table with this attractive orange place mat.

7 Should you wish to paint a sliced orange, cut open a real one and study it. Take a good look at the different segments of the orange before you paint them. Use a mixture of golden yellow, primrose yellow and magenta in the slices to create light and shade effects.

8 Paint the white part of the rind and the membranes between the segments with opaque white.

pears

Like oranges, pears are usually used in combination with other fruits (see examples on pages 22 and 53), but they also look very effective on their own.

PAINT
YELLOW: golden yellow
TRANSPARENT BASE: extender
GREEN: bright green
MAGENTA: magenta
BROWN: brown

BLENDS

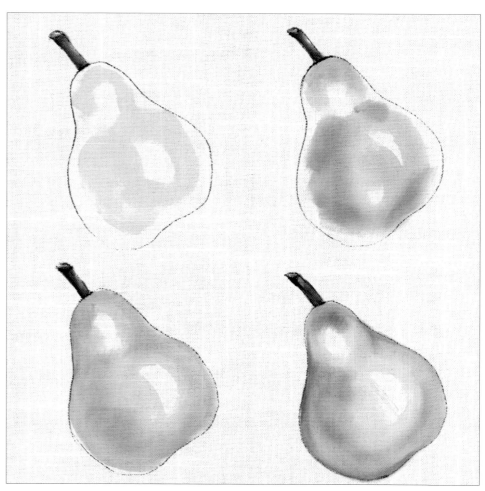

Start with the lighter colours so that the darker shades can be subtly blended in.

1 Using a black pen, trace the outlines of the design (see page 117) onto the fabric.

2 For the highlighted areas, decide where the light is going to fall on the pear so that the white of the fabric can be left open in that area.

3 Mix a little golden yellow with transparent base to get a very pale yellow and paint around the highlights. Paint quite a large area with this yellow because you can always make it darker.

4 Paint around the light yellow parts with golden yellow.

5 Mix a little bright green with golden yellow to create a lime green, and paint the remainder of the pear, especially along the outside edge.

6 Paint bright green right around the outer edges.

The darker shades used for the pear in the background give the design depth and accentuate the three-dimensional effect.

7 If the light falls from the right, you can paint the left-hand side a little darker than the right-hand side by mixing bright green or yellow with magenta.

8 Paint the stems using brown for the darker areas and ochre (a mixture of yellow and magenta) for the lighter areas.

IF YOU WANT TO PAINT BROWNER PEARS, ADD A LITTLE MAGENTA TO THE SHADES OF YELLOW AND THE MIXTURE OF YELLOW AND GREEN.

BASIC DESIGNS

grapes

There are many grape cultivars – each individual grape having its own unique colour, shape and size. In this book only variations of 'blue' grapes have been used, since the colours form such a marvellous contrast to other fruit, and blend in so well.

PAINT

BLUE: navy
MAGENTA: magenta
TRANSPARENT BASE: extender
GREEN: bright green,
   emerald green
YELLOW: primrose yellow

BLENDS

Notice how the colours are applied one at a time when painting grapes.

1 Using a black pen, trace the outlines of the design (see page 118) onto the fabric.

2 Mix different shades of blue and purple using navy, magenta and base in different proportions to each other.

3 Decide from which angle the light is going to fall on the grapes. In this example the light falls in front from the right. The grapes on the left will therefore have no highlights – only lighter areas. Decide which of the grapes on the right should reflect light and thus have a white highlight.

4 Paint around the highlights with a very light shade. When you paint round objects, the brush strokes must also be curved and without any sharp angles or straight lines.

5 Make sure that the colour of the grapes on the left and at the back of the bunch is always darker than that used on the right and at the top of the bunch.

6 Paint the leaves. Refer to pages 46–47 for a detailed explanation.

A completed bunch of grapes with leaves.

vine leaves

Leaves complement flowers or fruit. Vine leaves have been chosen as an example because they have such interesting shapes and colours. Any other leaves are painted in the same way – just adapt the shape and colour. Remember to study a couple of real leaves before you start to draw and paint. Compare the difference in shape, colour and texture of old and young leaves, as well as the difference in shades of colour on any single leaf. Take a good look at the young, green shoots and older, dry vines and stalks.

PAINT
GREEN: bright green,
  emerald green
YELLOW: primrose yellow
TRANSPARENT BASE: extender
BLUE: navy
BROWN: dark brown

BLENDS

These steps illustrate how the colours are applied one by one when you paint leaves.

This example covers how to paint a single leaf as well as how to expand the technique for painting an overlay covered with leaves.

1 Using a black pen, trace the large leaves in the foreground of the desgin onto the fabric. The leaves right at the back should not be outlined. They should be painted in with a brush to create the illusion that they are farther away in the background.

2 Mix at least five shades of green before you start painting.

3 Use bright green mixed with primrose yellow and transparent base to get the palest lime green; thereafter mix only base with green to get the other light shades of green.

4 Use emerald green, and a mixture of emerald green and navy to create the darker colours.

5 Paint in the leaves at the back with a brush, using a very pale green that almost seems yellow.

Leaves look so marvellous on their own that you can paint a whole article with leaves only. In the example above, an illusion of depth has been created by using different colours and shades of green, and large and small leaves.

6 First paint the palest colours on the leaves in the front. Also leave a lot of white fabric open along the edges of the leaves – this helps to lift out the front leaves. Gradually use darker colours towards the inside of the leaves and also from the front to the back of the leaves.

7 Paint the tender, delicate tendrils in shades of green and the thicker, harder shoots in shades of brown.

8 A medium shade of green looks wonderful as a border on the overlay, or it can be used for the background.

stripes and checks

Checks, stripes and blocks can be used on their own or in combination with other designs. Colours on opposite sides of the colour wheel, such as green and orange, make good colour combinations.

Make your own checked pattern and use it on its own or together with other designs.

1 The choice of fabric is very important when you are painting stripes or blocks. On some fabrics there are lovely clear lines, but on others the paint 'bleeds' and you will never get clean, sharp lines. You should therefore choose your fabric according to the effect you want to achieve.

2 On a sheet of paper, first plan the layout of the stripes, that is to say, the width and colours.

3 Masking tape should be used as a guide to get clean, neat lines when you paint, so plan the stripes according to the available widths of the masking tape.

4 First stick on the four outlines of a block, and then all the horizontal lines.

5 To make the lines equal in width, neatly stick three pieces of masking tape right next to each other. Now lift the middle strip and stick it directly against the right-hand side of the third strip. Stick another strip of tape next to this, then lift the re-used strip again. Repeat the process until you have covered the whole section.

6 Make sure that the masking tape is securely stuck down, otherwise the paint will seep in under the tape and you won't get clean, straight lines.

7 Mix enough paint in advance to complete the project in one sitting because here it is essential that the colours remain the same throughout.

Use checks like these on the backs of place mats.

8 Paint all the horizontal lines with a brush or scraper. Leave them to dry completely before you start sticking strips of masking tape in a vertical direction to create blocks.

9 Since the colours are transparent, the stripes should stop at the edge of the design, otherwise they will show through and spoil the effect.

combinations

WALL PANEL WITH
LEMON AND SUNFLOWER

PAINT

MAGENTA: magenta
YELLOW: primrose yellow, golden yellow
BROWN: dark brown
RED: brilliant red
BLUE: navy, royal blue
TRANSPARENT BASE: extender
GREEN: bright green, emerald green
WHITE: opaque white

1 For this example the designs (page 116 and 115) were enlarged approximately 10 times. The size of the finished wall panel is 60 x 60 cm (24 x 24 in).

2 Using a black pen, trace the outlines of the design onto the fabric.

3 Paint the lemon (see page 39) and the sunflower (see page 37).

4 Remember opaque white is only used for the white of the lemon rind.

5 Paint the background royal blue.

TABLECLOTH WITH
LEMONS IN SHADES OF BLUE

Any of the basic designs can be painted in shades of another colour. In this case blue lemons have been used as an example. Refer to page 1 to see the full design.

PAINT

BLUE: navy
TRANSPARENT BASE: extender

1 Using a black pen, trace the outlines of the design (see page 116) onto the fabric.

2 Mix four shades of blue paint which differ equally from each other in intensity. To do this, imagine that one end of the colour spectrum is white and the other end dark blue, with three other shades of blue in between.

3 Start with the lightest colour paint and add the other shades of blue as you would if you were painting a lemon (see page 39). It may feel strange at first to paint a blue lemon, but once you have made the first few brush strokes and start concentrating on the light and dark areas to achieve a three-dimensional effect, you'll quickly forget about the colour.

The unusual colour combination of this tablecloth's design would be very well suited to a blue-and-white colour scheme.

combinations

LARGE TABLECLOTH WITH FRUIT

The design for this tablecloth is composed of fruits that have already been dealt with in this chapter. Refer to page 68 to see the full design.

PAINT

FRUIT: use colours as indicated with each fruit

1 For this example the designs were enlarged about 10 times. The tablecloth measures 150 x 250 cm (60 x 98 in).

2 Once the designs have been enlarged, trace them onto the fabric using a black pen.

3 Because the areas to be painted are so large, you must mix enough paint of each colour for the whole tablecloth. This project will not be able to be completed in a day, but try for instance to paint all the yellow sections in one day. Take care not to smudge the paint when you are working.

4 Paint each different fruit as explained on pages 32–47.

5 Start painting in the middle of the tablecloth and work gradually towards the outside.

6 Finally paint the outside edge using an old X-ray film and a scraper (see page 28).

TEA COSY WITH FRUIT

The design on this tea cosy is composed of all the different fruits which have already been dealt with individually. A design like this can be enlarged and used on a tablecloth or even on curtains for a kitchen. This particuluar example has been quilted (see pages 88–90), which immediately gives depth to the fruit.

PAINT

FRUIT: use colours as indicated with each fruit
BLUE: royal blue
TRANSPARENT BASE: extender

1 Using a black pen, trace the outlines of the designs (see pages 112–118) onto the fabric.

2 Paint each of the fruits as explained on pages 32–47.

3 The background colour is obtained by mixing royal blue and a little base.

This is a lovely example of a composite design of fruit. With your knowledge of painting you, too, can paint such a masterpiece.

Advanced designs

This chapter deals with designs that are a bit more difficult than those in the previous chapter. If you've worked through the basic designs, however, you ought to have no problems. By this stage you would most probably have bought a couple of extra colours of paint and would be working on cultivating your own style. The examples in this chapter are not discussed as fully as in the previous chapter and some of the designs are not included in the book. You can, however, easily draw these on your own.

pumpkin

The rich blends of yellow make this pumpkin (see page 109) look good enough to eat!

PAINT
YELLOW: golden yellow,
primrose yellow
MAGENTA: magenta
BROWN: dark brown
RED: brilliant red

1 Using a black pen, trace the outlines of the design onto the fabric.

2 Paint the whole design with transparent paint and leave the natural white of the fabric for the skin and pips.

3 Use golden yellow for the flesh of the pumpkin, and magenta mixed with golden yellow for the shadows.

4 Use brown, primrose yellow and a little red for the background.

beetroot

This beetroot (see page 54) is painted with glowing, rich colours.

PAINT
YELLOW: primrose yellow
MAGENTA: magenta
BLUE: navy, royal blue
GREEN: brilliant green,
emerald green
PURPLE: violet

1 This design (see page 119) was enlarged about 10 times. The completed wall panel measures 60 x 60 cm (24 x 24 in).

2 Using a black pen, trace the outlines of the design onto the fabric.

3 Use a mixture of yellow and magenta to paint around the highlight, and shades of navy and magenta for the rest of the beetroot.

4 Mix five shades of green for the leaves. Use combinations of navy, yellow, and the two different greens. Use shades of the same colour that was used for the beetroot itself to paint the veins on the leaves.

5 Use a mixture of royal blue and violet for the background.

pea pod

This design can be painted on its own or in combination with other vegetables (see page 110).

PAINT
BLUE: navy
YELLOW: primrose yellow
GREEN: brilliant green,
emerald green
TRANSPARENT BASE: extender

1 The design in this example (see page 112) was enlarged approximately 10 times. The size of the finished panel is 60 x 60 cm (24 x 24 in).

2 Using a black pen, trace the outlines of the design onto the fabric.

3 Mix five different shades of green and use lots of transparent base to lighten the colours and paint from the lightest area to the darkest area. Paint in the shadows to create depth.

4 Use emerald green for the background.

mushroom

Mushrooms (see page 110) are fun to paint, especially if you like earthy colours.

PAINT
BROWN: golden brown
YELLOW: primrose yellow
TRANSPARENT BASE: extender
GREEN: emerald green

1 The design (see page 112) should be enlarged approximately 10 times. The size of the completed wall panel is 60 x 60 cm (24 x 24 in).

2 Using a black pen, trace the outlines of the design onto the fabric.

3 Use mixtures of brown and yellow with lots of transparent base for the different light brown colours.

4 Use emerald green for the background.

ADVANCED DESIGNS

tomatoes

Since there are so many different varieties and, depending on their ripeness, so many different colours of tomato, this can be a very interesting theme to use.

PAINT

TRANSPARENT BASE: extender
YELLOW: primrose yellow
RED: brilliant red
MAGENTA: magenta
BLUE: navy
GREEN: bright green

1 Using a black pen, trace the outlines of the design (see page 119) onto the fabric.

2 Decide where the highlights on the tomatoes should be and leave these areas open on the fabric. If you use the design on a tablecloth, make sure that the highlights are placed so that, depending from which side you look at the tablecloth, the light falls from above on each tomato (see accompanying illustration). It should therefore look more or less the same from any side. The front tomato is the lightest, the one just behind it a little darker and the tomato at the back the darkest.

The natural white of the fabric creates a more natural, subtle highlight than using opaque white paint.

3 Mix the colours by adding a lot of transparent base and yellow to the red, and then gradually making it darker. The red and magenta paints can also be mixed together as an intermediate colour. Mix magenta and navy for the shadows on the tomato.

4 Start painting with the lightest colours and then with the darker colours.

5 To paint the leaves, mix green with yellow for the lighter areas, then add navy for the darker areas in the middle of the leaves.

lavender

It is once again very fashionable to have lavender in the garden and, together with white roses, it seems all the more charming. Use your fabric remnants and paint sprigs of lavender on them, then use these bits of fabric to make lavender bags or covers for hangers.

PAINT
GREEN: bright green, emerald green
BLUE: navy
BLACK: black
MAGENTA: magenta
TRANSPARENT BASE: extender

1 Using a black pen, trace the outlines of the design onto the fabric.

2 Mix four different shades of green for the stems and leaves. If you want to make the leaves more grey-green, you can add a little navy or black.

3 Use three different shades of purple for the lavender flowers. Mix magenta and navy together and add transparent base to get the different shades.

A sprig of lavender on a remnant of fabric can easily be made up into a lavender bag.

hydrangeas

The colours of hydrangea flowers vary from almost completely white to different shades of pink, blue and purple. A young bud is painted in the first example. The florets are very pale and so the white of the fabric is used to depict this. Just a little yellow, green and blue are used to indicate depth.

PAINT

BLUE: navy
MAGENTA: magenta
TRANSPARENT BASE: extender
YELLOW: primrose yellow
GREEN: bright green,
  emerald green

Use bright green and pale blue around the edges to enhance the shape of the flowers.

1 Using a black pen, trace the outlines of the design (see page 120) onto the fabric.

2 The different colours of the flowers are obtained by mixing navy and magenta with base and with each other. To get an apricot purplish pink, mix a little yellow with magenta.

3 Use a mixture of bright green, base and yellow for the leaves, and emerald green mixed with navy for a darker green.

4 Use yellow in the middle of each young floret. Then use a little yellow-green and bright green and lots of pale blue to indicate shadows where the florets lie on top of each other. Also use it around the edges of the florets to create the effect of a round bush.

5 When you paint a more mature flower, paint the middle of each individual floret yellow too.

6 The florets in the centre at the top should be the lightest and should also be painted first.

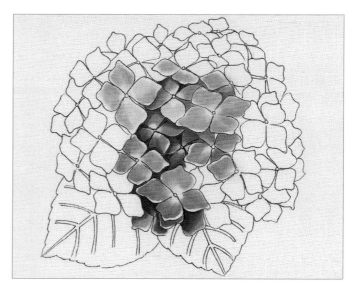

Notice the difference in colour between the different florets.

Hardly any paint is needed when painting flowers that are starting to bloom as they are very pale, delicate and small.

7 Gradually darken the colour of the florets towards the back.

8 Leave areas of white on the edges of the petals to lift out each floret and to give depth to the whole flower.

9 When you are painting a whole bunch of flowers with leaves, the light falls mostly on the foremost flowers and leaves, so these should be painted in the lightest colours.

10 Not all the leaves are drawn on the diagram and more leaves must be painted in on the outer edges of the design. The illusion must be created that they are farther away.

11 If possible, try to study the shape and texture of a real hydrangea leaf before you start painting. The veins must be visible on the front leaves, but farther towards the back the leaves become simpler in shape and texture.

pansies

Pansies are among the most cheerful and delightful of flowers to paint. This example is blue and purple, but you can paint yellow, white or even purplish pink flowers. If you decide to paint pansies, look at a real flower or study a drawing before you begin to paint.

PAINT

YELLOW: primrose yellow
BLUE: navy
PURPLE: purple
TRANSPARENT BASE: extender
WHITE: opaque white
GREEN: bright green,
    emerald green
GOLD: metallic gold
BORDER: navy

1 Using a blue pen, trace the outlines of the design (see page 121) onto the fabric.

2 First paint all the mouths of the flowers in shades of yellow and a mixture of yellow and purple.

3 For the hearts of the flowers use a mixture of blue and purple. Allow this paint to dry before you start using the other colours.

4 When the dark paint is dry, start painting all the different shades of blue. You get these different shades by mixing navy with base each time. Think of folded fabric when you paint the different shades of blue. The folds are usually light on top, and where the folds lie under each other they are dark.

5 Now paint the white parts of the petals around the dark parts with opaque white. If you feel there is too much blue, some of these parts can be painted out with the white. It also looks pretty if a little yellow is mixed into the white.

6 Mix five different shades of green for the leaves:
- bright green, yellow and base for the lightest green;
- bright green and base for the light green;
- bright green on its own;
- bright green and emerald green for a darker green;
- emerald green and navy for the darkest green.

7 Pansy leaves fold away to the back with the result that the light does not fall on the edges of the leaves, as is the case with other leaves, but on the curves. Try to capture the curves of the leaves. Study the leaves very well and decide which ones are going to lie in front and which to the back. The leaves at the back are very dark and those in front lighter. Some leaves are also younger than others and thus lighter in colour. Again start painting the lightest part of the leaves first. Remember to make the brush strokes in the direction of the grain of the leaves.

8 Use a gold outliner on the edges of the petals to emphasize the flowers.

9 If you decide to make a tablecloth, finish it off with a double blue border to enhance the design. Use a mixture of navy and extender for the lighter border and navy for the darker border. Make sure that the light blue border is completely dry before you begin to scrape the dark blue border (refer to page 28).

Gold outliner can be used to highlight the pansies. This also gives the design a professional finish.

poinsettias & holly

Poinsettias and holly are associated with Christmas and nowadays also with Easter. Make a special overlay and matching serviettes, using a green background for Christmas and a white background for Easter.

PAINT

BLUE: navy
MAGENTA: magenta
YELLOW: primrose yellow
RED: brilliant red
GREEN: bright green,
   emerald green
TRANSPARENT BASE: extender

In this example the background has been scraped with bright green, and a dark green border has been added to complete the design.

1 Using a black pen, trace the outlines of the design (see page 119) onto the fabric.

2 Leave the middle or main vein of each petal white. Mix navy and magenta together and use it to paint the other veins as well as the dark shadows where the petals cross each other.

3 Start painting the petals from the top to the bottom. For a three-dimensional effect, the petals at the top should be the lightest and should contain the most yellow. The closer the leaves are placed to the bottom, the more red and later magenta should be added. For the darkest areas even more magenta and navy should be added.

4 Finish off each petal with a reddish yellow or pink, but remember to leave a white highlight on each one.

5 Now paint the large main veins of the petals with light orange.

6 Use the same method to paint the leaves, but here use a mixture of emerald green and navy to paint the veins on the leaves. Paint the rest of the leaves with lighter shades of green and leave white strips open along the edges of the leaves.

7 Holly is done in the same way and with the same colours as poinsettias – there are just berries instead of leaves.

This Christmas overlay with holly uses the same colours as the poinsettia.

Notice how the different colours are applied to the petals one after the other until the desired effect is achieved.

roses

For a more traditional design, roses have been included. Experiment with the designs at the back of the book and compose your own designs.

PAINT

YELLOW: primrose yellow
MAGENTA: magenta
TRANSPARENT BASE: extender
BLUE: navy
GREEN: bright green,
   emerald green

1 In this example the design (see page 122) was enlarged 10 times and then used to create a composition of roses.

2 Using a red outliner or fabric marker, trace the outlines of the design onto the fabric. The leaves at the back should only be painted and not drawn with the pen. Also make these leaves smaller and use lighter colours than for the others.

3 Before you start painting, have a good look at a real rose to get a feeling for these flowers. Rose petals have a very smooth texture and so are painted very evenly in contrast with the green leaves that are painted with streaks. The petals of a rose are usually also curly so that there are interesting light and dark areas to depict.

4 For the apricot-pink mix yellow and magenta with a lot of base.

5 When you paint the background, you can use different blues, greens and yellows to create the illusion that it is a real bunch of flowers in nature. Don't be afraid of using very dark and very light colours to achieve depth.

> MAKE SURE THAT YOUR BRUSHES ARE CLEAN BEFORE YOU BEGIN TO PAINT, PARTICULARLY IF YOU ARE USING A LIGHT COLOUR. THE REMAINS OF ANOTHER COLOUR CAN CHANGE THE COLOUR OF YOUR PAINT AND SPOIL YOUR WORK.

For a classic look, combine a traditional design with subtle colours such as apricot and pink.

Composite designs

This chapter briefly discusses a few designs which include compositions of simple and

advanced designs. The diagrams for these designs are not included, the idea being that

when you have worked through the previous chapters you will have the self-confidence to

create your own unique designs, with a little help from the accompanying notes. The key

to success is planning and preparation. Carefully consider the composition of the design

and plan how you are going to create depth and perspective. Some of the colours indicated

are ready-mixed, since those who tackle projects like these usually have a collection of

colours. If this is not the case, the colours can still be made by mixing the basic colours.

basket with fruit

This versatile pattern can be used for place mats, tea cosies and other articles.

PAINT

YELLOW: golden yellow
MAGENTA: magenta
TRANSPARENT BASE: extender
GREEN: bright green
GOLD: metallic gold
BLUE: navy
BROWN: dark brown
RED: brilliant red
WHITE: opaque white

1 Using a black pen, trace the outlines of the design (see page 126) onto the fabric.

2 Paint the border pattern and basket with fruit. Use the colours as indicated in chapter two (see pages 31–53) for the different fruits, and use various shades of brown for the basket. Leave the paint to dry completely before you commence with the following step.

3 Now stick four strips of masking tape very firmly onto the fabric in a square around the central design. Stick another four strips to the inside of the border pattern to form two square blocks. In other words, the basket should be positioned within the central square and the border design should be outside the second square. Remember that the strips of masking tape end where they intersect each other at right angles.

4 Mix cream-coloured paint by mixing a little yellow with magenta and lots of base. Make certain that the paint is well mixed so that it doesn't create streaks. To avoid differences in colour, see that you mix enough paint for the whole area.

5 Now scrape the cream-coloured paint over all the painted areas, that is to say, in the central block and also around the border. This layer of paint gives the whole tablecloth a look of times gone by.

6 Scrape a green border around the outer edge of the tablecloth.

7 Outline all the edges of the design and the squares in gold.

8 Complete the tablecloth by overlocking the edges with green thread.

The natural colours and composite design of this tablecloth make it ideal for use in a rustic or outdoor setting.

shells & sea urchins

The sea with its great variety of plants, animals and shells offers a host of objects to paint. There are quite a few designs of different shells and sea urchins at the back of the book (see page 123) and you can use them to compose your own designs. The colours used here are very subtle and unusual; many different shades of light brown and light ochre can be used, particularly for the sand.

PAINT

BLUE: navy, royal blue
TURQUOISE: turquoise
YELLOW: primrose yellow
MAGENTA: magenta
GREEN: bright green
TRANSPARENT BASE: extender
WHITE: opaque white
GOLD: metallic gold

1 Using a black pen, trace the outlines of the design onto the fabric.

2 Divide the background into three – a broad middle area and two narrow strips on the side. Paint the middle area lighter than the two outer strips. Use variations of the two blues and turquoise for the background. To get the sand colours, mix a little yellow and magenta with a lot of base. Add more yellow to get the beige colours, and more magenta for the dirty pink colours.

3 For the brownish shells, mix four different shades with magenta and a lot of yellow, and another four shades with yellow and a lot of magenta. For the greyish shells, dilute navy with a lot of base. For the sea urchins, mix four different shades of green by adding yellow, navy and base. The sea urchins can also be painted in shades of blue or purple.

4 Small quantities of paint can be mixed with water and splashed onto the background to represent splashes of water.

5 Use opaque white for the inside of the shells and gold to add a decorative touch.

This fetching wall panel would look right at home in a bathroom.

tablecloth with roses

Thorough planning and patience are needed to paint a tablecloth like this one. As it is so large, you must see to it that you have enough space in which to work and that you mix sufficient paint to finish everything, otherwise the colours on one side of the tablecloth may differ from those on the other side. Any combination of colours can be used.

PAINT

YELLOW: primrose yellow
BROWN: dark brown
BLACK: black
TRANSPARENT BASE: extender
RED: brilliant red
WHITE: opaque white

1 Plan the layout very carefully on paper before you buy fabric or paint. For such a large tablecloth the design of the flowers, in this case iceberg roses, will have to be enlarged. Decide how big they should be and enlarge them either electronically or by using a grid.

2 Wash and iron the fabric and see that it is cut square to the right size.

3 Using a black pen, trace the outlines of the flowers onto the fabric.

4 Mark the areas that are going to be scraped, in this case the roses, by very carefully sticking down masking tape.

5 Mix the following three colours of paint as follows:
 ✤ **Ochre:** yellow and brown with a trace of black and base
 ✤ **Rust:** red, yellow and brown
 ✤ **Grey:** black and base

6 Using broad strokes, scrape the three colours over all the roses so that they sometimes overlap and are sometimes single-layered. When you scrape, always scrape away from the masking tape to the inside. Make sure that the paint does not seep in under the tape and spoil the effect. Allow the paint to dry very well before you proceed.

7 Now write the words on the fabric with a permanent marker or outliner. If you are nervous about writing directly onto the fabric, first write on paper and then trace the writing onto the fabric using a light-table. Let it dry before painting the background.

8 Use masking tape to mark off the grey areas and scrape this paint onto the fabric. Allow the paint to dry very well before you paint the dark grey border.

9 Paint the dark grey border with a scraper and an X-ray film (see page 28).

10 Finally give the tablecloth a nice finish by over-painting the roses with opaque white paint and a mixture of opaque white and base. Try to lift out the most important petals by painting the opaque white from the outside inwards. The white can also be mixed with any of the three colours to accentuate the underlying scraped colours.

The scraping technique and an inspirational quote lend a personal touch to this elegant tablecloth.

blind with vegetables

Blinds can serve a dual purpose – as a window covering and as a painting. The only disadvantage is that the whole pattern cannot be seen clearly when the blind is rolled up. Here, the vegetables, fruit and flowers were chosen so that their natural colours would harmonize with a terracotta colour scheme. The finished blind measures 94 x 150 cm (37 x 60 in).

PAINT

YELLOW: primrose yellow
MAGENTA: magenta
BROWN: dark brown
WHITE: opaque white
TRANSPARENT BASE: extender

1 Plan the design and enlarge it electronically or by redrawing with a grid to the desired size.

2 Using a black pen, trace the outlines of the design onto the fabric.

3 Ochre and terracotta are created by mixing yellow and magenta. The more yellow and less magenta, the more ochre the colour will be. The more magenta and less yellow, the more terracotta the colour will be. In this example, about three shades each of ochre, terracotta and brown are used. Add extender to create lighter shades.

4 Use opaque white only for the inside of the orange rind.

5 Leave large patches of white open on the fabric to allow light to filter through when the blinds are drawn.

Using a large design on a blind will make a small kitchen or room look bigger.

arum lilies

The following examples show how using two different paint techniques result in two different end products. For the first example a painting technique is used, and for the second a paint-and-scrape technique is used.

The design

1 Use the designs at the back of the book (see page 124) to assemble the design. The position of the leaves and flowers is very important and should form a whole, so start with the flowers when you start drawing.

2 The flowers should fit easily into the framework.

3 Make certain that all the leaves and flowers are clearly recognizable when you look at them.

4 It's not necessary to draw in all the leaves when you make up the design. The leaves at the back are just painted in at the end. For this example only five flowers and five leaves have been drawn on the design.

Painting technique

Follow the basic guidelines for the painting technique (see pages 22–23).

PAINT

GREEN: bright green, emerald green
YELLOW: primrose yellow
TRANSPARENT BASE: extender
BLUE: navy
MAGENTA: magenta
WHITE: opaque white

1 Using a black pen, trace the outlines of the design onto the fabric.

2 Study a real arum leaf and flower before you start painting. Note the texture and grain of the leaves and the light and shadow – this will give depth and shape to the work.

3 The most important colour in this painting is green. Mix bright green, a little yellow and a lot of base for the lightest green. Mix other shades of green by adding less and less base and so making them darker. For the darkest green, add navy to emerald green.

4 Begin by painting the lightest green on the leaves and stems of the flowers and gradually build up to the darkest greens on the leaves at the back.

5 Paint a lot of detail into the leaves in the foreground and make the leaves in the background more simple.

6 Make a few light colours from mixtures of navy, magenta, yellow and lots of transparent base. Use these colours for the shadows on the flowers to create a three-dimensional effect.

7 The background is filled in with many light spots. Use light greens to indicate leaves that are disappearing in the background and pale blues to represent the light.

8 Lastly paint the white parts of the flowers with opaque white paint.

THE WHITE OPAQUE PAINT AND MIXTURES OF IT ARE USED ONLY FOR PAINTING THE FLOWERS.

These arum lilies were done using the painting technique. Notice how the shadows on the flowers are painted with a light mixture of navy, magenta and yellow. You can also use a little green for the bases of the flowers.

arum lilies

Scraping technique

Use the basic guidelines for the scraping technique (see page 27).

PAINT

YELLOW: primrose yellow
BROWN: dark brown
BLACK: black
TRANSPARENT BASE: extender
RED: brilliant red
WHITE: opaque white

1 Using a black pen, trace the outlines of the design onto the fabric.

2 Make sure that the outlines are dry before you begin to apply the paint as they can easily smudge when using this technique.

3 Mix four colours for the scraping technique:

❖ A mixture of yellow, a little brown, a little black and lots of base;
❖ A mixture of yellow, a little brown, a little black and less base;
❖ A mixture of yellow, red, brown and transparent base;
❖ A mixture of black and base.

4 Using a scraper, scrape the different colours over the line drawing. Use the lightest colours at the top and on the outside of the design and the dark colours in the middle and at the bottom.

5 Paint the flowers with opaque white diluted with base while the other colours are still wet. The opaque white is diluted with base so that it doesn't look as though it has been pasted on top, but gradually blends in with the other colours.

6 Paint some of the colours used in the scraping on the leaves as well as directly outside the flowers and leaves to achieve more depth.

> CLEAN THE SCRAPER WELL EACH TIME BEFORE YOU USE A NEW COLOUR. IF THERE IS EVEN ONE GRAIN OF OLD, DRY PAINT STUCK TO IT, IT WILL MAKE A MARK ON YOUR WORK WHEN IT BECOMES WET WITH THE NEW PAINT.

This design is the same as in the previous example, but a completely different effect has been created by using the scraping technique.

wall panel or blind

This design is quite different from what you have done up to now. It has been included to show that you can break away completely from the traditional by drawing other kinds of objects, using strange colours and metallic paint, and even combining a bit of wisdom within the painting.

PAINT

BLUE: navy
YELLOW: primrose yellow
GREEN: bright green
MAGENTA: magenta
PURPLE: violet
BLACK: black
TRANSPARENT BASE: extender
BRONZE: metallic bronze
GOLD: metallic gold

1 Use two different outliners to transfer the design onto the fabric: black for the front and most important objects, and grey for the less obvious objects towards the back.

2 Make quite sure that the outlines of the design are dry before you start painting. Paint the background by scraping the different transparent colours over each other. Start with the lightest colours and gradually progress to the darker colours.

3 Paint in the detail of the fruit and the dish with a brush. Use a gold and bronze outliner to emphasize the prescribed areas and the edges of the fruit and leaves.

4 The quotation on this particular painting is the following: 'The artist is the person who makes life more interesting or beautiful, more understandable or mysterious, or probably, in the best sense more wonderful.' George Bellows (1882–1925), from *Art Lovers' Quotations* (ed. Helen Exley).

5 Paint the large gold and bronze areas with a brush.

DESIGNS LIKE THESE CAN EVEN BE PAINTED DIRECTLY ON INSIDE AND OUTSIDE WALLS. MIX ORDINARY PVA PAINT WITH FABRIC PAINT SO THAT THE PAINT DOESN'T WASH OFF TOO EASILY. THE GOLD AND BRONZE LOOK PARTICULARLY BEAUTIFUL ON A WALL.

"The artist is the person who makes
life more interesting or beautiful,
more understandable or mysterious,
or probably in the best sense,
more wonderful."
George Bellows
(1882–1925)

*A design like this is equally
effective on a wall panel or blind.*

view through a window

To complete a project like this successfully, careful planning is needed. This example took a long time of plotting and playing on paper. The wooden shutters and window frames were first drawn on paper and then the landscape and all the detail were added. Many of the leaves were not originally on the design, but only filled in later with a brush.

PAINT

BLUE: navy
OCHRE: mustard
GREEN: bright green
PURPLE: violet
WHITE: opaque white
TRANSPARENT BASE: extender

1 Use a black pen or outliner to trace the outlines of the design onto the fabric. Outline only the leaves in the foreground, and paint in the background leaves with a brush later on.

2 First paint the window frame and shutters. Wherever possible, use scrapers and then round off with a brush. Use very 'loose' brush strokes here to indicate the texture of the wood.

3 Paint the curtain with a brush and let the strokes of the brush follow the direction of the folds to give them depth and texture.

4 Paint the background of the scene within the window frame. Here, too, use the brush strokes to give depth and texture to the sky and plants.

5 Paint the detail, such as the pot plants in the foreground, using darker colours than those in the background to create the illusion that the landscape disappears into the distance.

6 When you have finished painting the whole scene in the window frame, use some opaque white diluted with lots of base to paint over it. This will create the illusion of glass in the window frame. Be careful, however, not to paint away the background of the scene in the window frame by using too much white paint.

7 Partially paint the flowers and flower pots with undiluted opaque white paint.

8 Finally round off the article with an even ochre colour all around the window. Use scrapers and sponges for this, except in the places where the background touches the shutters and window-sill. Here you must use a brush to make neat and clear divisions.

Give a small urban apartment the illusion of a country vista with this decorative wall hanging.

Articles made with painted fabric

Among the most popular items made with painted fabric are tablecloths, place mats,

tea cosies, pot holders, aprons, wall panels and blinds. Articles that need wadding,

for example place mats, tea cosies and pot holders, are often quilted. This chapter

gives instructions for making quilted articles, as well as providing instructions for

making a variety of other useful articles.

MACHINE QUILTING

Tea cosies, place mats and pot holders look very professional when the wadding is quilted down. Not only does it make the article stronger, but it also adds texture to the painting.

COLOUR OF STITCHING

The colour of the stitching, like the colour of the outlining of a design, has a great influence on the appearance of the product. The usual colour for quilting is black, but it sometimes looks very hard. It can make a big difference when you use a colour like navy blue or bottle green for the quilting. A dark grey also sometimes looks better than black.

First test the colours on a separate bit of fabric since you can't pull it out once you have started with one colour. You can also get an interesting effect by quilting the outlines in different colours. The amount of quilting on an article will depend on personal preference and the effect you want to achieve. It isn't necessary to stitch on all the lines of the design. If you only want to strengthen the article with the stitching, you could stitch the outlines of the design only. But if you are looking for a more three-dimensional effect, then stitch on all the lines. A full design of fruit and flowers in particular looks wonderful when it is rounded off in this way.

If the tension of your machine is set perfectly, in other words when the upper thread and the lower thread connect precisely between the top and bottom of the stitching to form a stitch, it can also look very effective when you use one colour for the top thread and another colour for the lower thread on a finished article such as a place mat. But take care that the lower colour doesn't show on the top and vice versa. In this way the outline of the design can be executed on the plain back of a place mat, for instance. Just remember that it is a lot of work and very time-consuming to quilt an article. If you want to make articles for sale, you'll have to take this into consideration when you are calculating the price.

CHOICE OF WADDING (BATTING)

When an article has to be quilted, the choice of wadding is very important. Use a thick wadding for a tea cosy and a thinner, stiffer kind for place mats and pot holders. The thinner wadding looks a lot like felt and is often more difficult to find than the thicker, more loosely woven variety.

Sponge can also be used for place mats and pot holders when nothing else is available, but it is inclined to stick to the machine when you are quilting, and this usually happens exactly when you need to be able to move the article easily and freely. Sponge also easily hooks on the machine and tears, or tears when it is stitched back and forth. Wadding is longer lasting than sponge and is definitely the better option.

PACKETS OF FOUR OR SIX SERVIETTES WITH PLACE MATS WITHOUT WADDING AND QUILTING SELL VERY WELL AT MARKETS AND GIFT SHOPS. THEY DON'T TAKE VERY LONG TO MAKE AND THE FABRIC IS ALSO NOT VERY EXPENSIVE.

This lovely example shows how the fabric painting is complemented by the quilting. The stitching detail is also clearly visible on the underside of the place mat.

HOW TO USE
THE SEWING MACHINE

You don't need a fancy machine for quilting. It's actually quite fun if you can quilt with an old machine that's not too fussy, even an old hand-model will do. Set about quilting as follows:

1 Pin the front side of the article to be quilted, painted side up, on the wadding. Cut the wadding a couple of centimetres wider than the article.

2 Use a thick needle (no. 90 or 100) and the freehand embroidery foot of your machine. This foot looks like a round open circle which is attached to the metal rod of the foot.

3 Lower the feeding mechanism of the machine so that the article can move around freely.

4 Set the stitch length to fairly long. The length of the stitch will constantly change depending on how quickly you move the article under the foot.

5 Decide on the colour thread you intend using and see to it that the bottom bobbin is fully wound with this colour. If the thread at the bottom runs out suddenly or often, it can lead to a tangle which could spoil the article and which is often very difficult to unravel.

6 When the whole article is being quilted, for instance a place mat, you will first stitch the top to the wadding in just a few places, add the backing, finish the place mat and then quilt it. If only the top or front is being quilted, you usually start quilting in the middle and then work systematically outwards.

7 It's very difficult to unravel the stitching of quilting, particularly when it is stitched to thick wadding. If you try to unpick the stitching on a painted surface it will more than likely damage the paintwork and the thick needles will leave holes in the fabric which can't be repaired.

8 When you start quilting the design, work a couple of stitches backwards and forwards – this ensures that the stitching will not unravel later on. Now guide the fabric with wadding in the direction you wish to stitch. It's not necessary to stitch exactly on the lines because you are actually drawing with the needle too. First practise on another remnant of fabric before you start quilting the painted article. The 'looser' the stitching, in other words the more easily the fabric moves under the foot, the more beautiful the quilting. It all becomes much easier with practice.

9 When you are finishing off each section of the quilting, stitch back and forth a couple of times, but don't cut the thread each time. Lift up the foot of the machine and move the fabric to the place where you are going to begin stitching again. If you do choose to cut the thread every time you could easily work the loose threads into the following stitches. But be careful that the piece of thread between the two stitchings is not too short, as this could cause the fabric to pucker up.

10 When the quilting is finished, cut the threads very close to the fabric, first on the front and then on the back, using sharp pointed scissors.

11 Now press the article very well, but be careful that the wadding does not melt from the heat.

MAKING ARTICLES

Conventional methods don't always apply when making articles from painted fabric. The reason for this is that the old methods are often time-consuming or do not work as well, and if you are making articles to sell, time is a very important consideration. Nobody can really ever pay you adequately for the time that handwork demands, so time-effective methods are important. The methods used here are only suggestions and if you find a method that works better, do use it.

TABLECLOTHS AND SERVIETTES

Of all the articles made from painted fabric, tablecloths and serviettes are the easiest and most useful. Beginners therefore usually like to tackle a tablecloth as a first project.

The standard sizes for square tablecloths are 100 x 100 cm (39 x 39 in) for an overlay or 120 x 120 cm (47 x 47 in) for a tea cloth. If a cloth is being made for a specific table, take the measurements of the table and add 20–30 cm (8–12 in), depending on the size of the table, all round.

For a round table, measure the diameter of the table and divide by two. Add 20–30 cm (8–12 in) as overhang to get the radius of the tablecloth. To cut the tablecloth, fold the fabric precisely and neatly in half and then in half again so that it forms a square that is a quarter of the area of the whole table-cloth. The folded sides of the square can be folded over once more to form a triangle, but sometimes the fabric is then too thick to cut. Now fasten a piece of string to a pencil, making the string the same length as the radius of the tablecloth. Hold the end of the string at the folded point of the fabric, which is the centre of the tablecloth, while a second person draws a quarter circle on the fabric with the pencil. Cut out the tablecloth precisely on this line.

The sizes of serviettes vary, but 30 x 30 cm (12 x 12 in) for small serviettes and 40 x 40 cm (16 x 16 in) for larger serviettes can be used as a standard measure.

A plain strip of about 5 cm (2 in) painted around the edges of tablecloths or serviettes always looks good and gives the articles a lovely finish.

> DO YOU OWN A DINNER SERVICE WITH A UNIQUE DESIGN? MAKE A TABLECLOTH AND SERVIETTES TO MATCH. DRAW THE DESIGN ON PAPER, ENLARGE IT AND PAINT IT ON THE FABRIC.

Requirements
- Fabric for tablecloth (and serviettes, if so desired)
- Paint as required for each design
- Brushes
- Scrapers
- Old X-ray films
- Overlocker
- Thread in the colour of the paint used in the border

1 Measure the table and add 20–30 cm (8–12 in), depending on the size of the table, all round.

2 Calculate how much fabric you need and add around 10 per cent extra to allow for shrinkage if you are using fabric made of natural fibre.

3 Prepare the fabric by washing and ironing it.

4 Cut the fabric exactly square before you begin to apply the design. In the case of a tablecloth it is particularly important that it is square, otherwise the whole tablecloth will hang skew.

5 Trace the design onto the fabric, but keep the plain border in mind.

6 For a serviette, a small design in one corner looks very good, but you can also cover the whole serviette with a design, or paint it in a single colour.

7 Lay the tablecloth flat on a large table or even on the floor if you can't make another plan. However, it's not very comfortable crawling around on the floor while painting.

8 Paint the design, working from the inside outwards to prevent the paint from smudging.

9 Use a scraper to paint the plain border of about 5 cm (2 in) all round. Use the side of an old X-ray film as a guide for keeping the sides straight.

10 Let the paint dry completely before handling or folding the cloth. A tablecloth is usually very large and if you handle it while the paint is wet, you are bound to get smudges.

11 Fix the paint using any of the heat treatments described on page 29.

12 Only sew the hem after the heat treatment as the thread could easily melt in the oven. Using the overlocker, stitch a border of compact, 4 mm (³⁄₁₆ in) wide satin stitch that looks almost like the finish of a buttonhole. First test the stitching on a remnant of fabric before sewing the tablecloth.

13 If you don't have an overlocker, you can finish the edge with a 1 cm (³⁄₈ in) hem, but remember to include this hem when you are working out measurements, otherwise the tablecloth will end up smaller than planned.

> PAINT A WITTY SAYING, A PERSONAL MESSAGE
> OR QUOTATION ON A TABLECLOTH, APRON
> OR ANY OTHER ARTICLE TO MAKE IT SPECIAL
> AND MORE INTERESTING.

*The most popular items made from painted fabric
are tablecloths and serviettes.*

PLACE MATS

Place mats are among the most useful and satisfying articles to make. The mats can take any shape, for instance that of any fruit, flower or shell. The size of the mats may vary, but ensure that they are not too small to accommodate a plate.

Ordinary rectangular mats are also practical and serviceable. The completed size of rectangular place mats should generally be 28 x 42 cm (11 x 16½ in).

Requirements

- About 30 x 90 cm (12 x 36 in) densely woven fabric for an ordinary mat. You'll need 100 x 55 cm (39 x 22 in) for a mat in the shape of a fruit, for example an orange or lemon. Allow 10 per cent extra fabric for shrinkage. If the mat has a distinctive shape, you'll need more fabric. Make quite sure of the amount of fabric you need before buying it.
- Approximately 30 x 45 cm (12 x 18 in) thin, stiff wadding for a rectangular mat and 50 x 55 cm (20 x 22 in) for a mat with an irregular shape.
- Paint as required for the design
- Brushes
- Thread for quilting

1 Decide in advance on the completed size and the design. It can be interesting if the mats are not all exactly the same. The place mats could also have two different motifs, perhaps flowers on one side and fruit on the other side, but these can't be quilted right through.

2 Calculate how much fabric you will need and prepare it (see page 11).

Surprise your guests with fun, fruit-shaped place mats.

3 Cut the fabric into two rectangles (one for the front and one for the back of the mat), leaving enough fabric for hems.

4 Trace the designs onto the front of the mats and also trace the finished size of the mats to serve as a guideline.

5 Cut out the front of the mats, including a seam allowance of approximately 2 cm (¾ in).

6 Cut the backs the same size as the fronts.

7 Paint the design on the front. Make sure that the paint extends about 1 cm (⅜ in) over the guidline so that there will not be a white bit showing when the front and back are sewn together.

8 Paint the backs. These are usually painted in a single colour, most often the colour of the front's background, but stripes and checks (see page 48) also look good and can even be used for the top. If the place mats are shaped like a fruit, the back can be painted like the front, with highlights, but without leaves. Make sure that you paint a mirror image of the front if the mat is asymmetrical, or you'll end up with two fronts and no back.

9 Let the paint dry completely before proceeding. It usually takes a day, but in damp weather it may take even longer.

10 Fix the paint using one of the heat treatments described on page 29.

11 Pin the front of the mat to the wadding and cut the wadding to the same size as the mat plus seam allowance if you are not going to quilt it, and a little bigger than the mat if you are going to quilt it.

12 If you are going to quilt only the top of the mat, do this now (see page 90).

13 Stitch the top of the mat along the outline to serve as a guide for when you stitch the front and back together.

14 With right sides facing, neatly pin the back and the front together.

15 Stitch the two sides together along the guideline, with the wadding on the outside. Start and finish by sewing stitches back and forth a few times to prevent the stitching from unravelling. Leave an opening of about 8 cm (3¼ in) in the longest side, so that the mat can be turned inside out.

16 Snip the seam allowance to approximately 1 cm (⅜ in) wide all round.

17 Snip notches in the curves of the seam so that it will leave a neat, smooth curve when the place mat is turned inside out.

18 Turn the mat inside out and smooth out the corners with your fingers, working from the centre. Using invisible stitches, neatly close the opening.

19 Iron the mat with care.

20 If the quilting on the back of the place mat needs to be visible, do it now.

21 If the mat is not going to be quilted at all, you can stitch a line on top of the mat about 2 mm (1⁄16 in) from the edge to ensure that the mat is firm and lies flat.

TEA COSIES AND TRAY CLOTHS

A tea cosy and tray cloth always makes a great gift. Both can be quilted, or a design can just be painted on the fabric. Use the directions for a place mat to make a tray cloth.

Requirements

TEA COSY
- 70 x 90 cm (28 x 36 in) firm cotton fabric
- 2 pieces of thick wadding, 40 x 35 cm (16 x 14 in)
- Paint as required for the design
- Brushes
- Thread for quilting

1 Prepare the fabric as described on page 11.

2 Use the diagram of the tea cosy that appears on page 127 to make a pattern on paper. This pattern already makes allowance for seams.

3 Cut out four of these patterns from the fabric.

4 Trace the design on two of these pieces of fabric. If you prefer, you need only draw a design on the front of the tea cosy, but it's usually more striking when the pattern is painted on both sides. To make the tea cosy even more interesting, you could paint different designs on each side.

5 Paint the design and allow the paint to dry completely.

6 Paint the two pieces of fabric for the lining in a plain colour. A dark colour like deep blue or green looks stunning and is also very practical as it doesn't show the dirt easily.

7 Fix the paint using one of the heat treatments described on page 29.

8 Pin each piece of painted fabric to each piece of wadding, cutting the wadding a little larger than the fabric if you are going to quilt the design, or the same size if it is to be left plain.

9 If you are going to quilt the design, this is the time to do it. When you have completed the quilting, cut the wadding to the same size as the fabric.

10 With right sides facing, neatly and firmly pin the outer edges of the tea cosy together, placing pins vertically towards the outside edges of the wadding.

11 Stitch the two outsides and the wadding together with a seam 1 cm (⅜ in) in width. Keep the stitches fairly long and use a thick needle, but make sure that you work slowly and carefully to prevent the needle from breaking. Work evenly around the curves so that there will be a smooth curve when the tea cosy is turned inside out.

12 Snip notches in the seam allowance around the curves, turn the tea cosy right side out and smooth out the seam with your fingers.

13 Cut the two pieces of lining 3 cm (1¼ in) shorter than the original pattern so that the lining doesn't show after it is stitched. Because the wadding is very thick, the lining can't be pushed in right up against the outer seam of the tea cosy. Stitch the panels of the lining together with a seam 1 cm (⅜ in) in width.

14 Cut the seam allowance of the lining narrower and snip notches in the curves.

15 Pull the lining, with the right side inside, over the outside of the tea cosy, with the right side outside.

16 Very carefully pin the lower edges of the tea cosy and lining together, with the pins vertical to the edge. Make sure that the edges lie precisely on top of each other and stitch them together with a seam 1 cm (⅜ in) in width. Leave an opening of about 6 cm (2¼ in) at the back of the tea cosy so that it can be turned inside out. Remember that the outside with the padding, which is now inside, is bigger than the lining that now lies outside – this will be rectified when the tea cosy is turned right way out.

17 Turn the tea cosy right way out and sew the opening together with small overhand stitches.

18 Pin the outside of the tea cosy and the lining firmly together so that the outside folds over to the inside by about 2 mm (¹⁄₁₆ in). Again attach the pins vertically to the edge so that the top and bottom layers do not move when you stitch them together.

19 Using long stitches, sew a double layer of stitching about 1 cm (⅜ in) from the bottom edge on the outside of the tea cosy.

DRAW PATTERNS OF A TEA COSY AND A RECTANGULAR PLACE MAT ON PIECES OF CARDBOARD. TRANSFER THE PATTERNS TO THE FABRIC BY PULLING A PEN OR PENCIL AROUND THE CARDBOARD.

TOWELS

Buy a length of towelling and make these cute little towels as a gift for a kitchen tea.

Requirements
- 40 x 50 cm (16 x 20 in) towelling for each towel
- 13 x 42 cm (5¼ x 16½ in) fabric for painting on
- Overlocker
- Paint as required for the design
- Brushes

1 Cut the towelling very carefully into neat rectangles and use an overlocker to finish them with a 4 mm (³⁄₁₆ in) wide satin stitch that looks like the finish of a buttonhole. First test the stitching on another scrap of fabric.

2 Using a black pen, carefully trace the design onto the fabric to be painted.

3 Paint the design and let it dry completely.

4 Fix the paint using one of the heat treatments described on page 29.

5 Overlock the painted fabric with a dense 4 mm (³⁄₁₆ in) wide satin stitch. First test the stitching on another scrap of fabric before you stitch around your painted fabric.

6 Stitch the fabric onto the towel around the edge using straight stitches and then a zig-zag stitch. You can also fold in a 1 cm (⅜ in) hem and then stitch the fabric to the towel.

This matching set will suit a blue or yellow colour scheme.

TEA SHOWERS

Make a tea shower that matches your tablecloth and serviettes and that looks a little different to the usual netting that is finished with a lace border. You could even be more adventurous and use a dark colour netting, for instance a bright green or purple, instead of the usual white or off-white. These two colours look particularly striking with a border pattern of grapes or fruit. If not available, you could use Terylene™ or French voile for the inside section.

It is preferable to finish the shower and then do the painting rather than the other way around, as it sometimes happens that the motifs don't come out directly in the centre of a side, no matter how carefully you have measured.

Requirements
- Coloured or white net, large enough to cover the top of the table
- Strips of coloured or white fabric 14 cm (5½ in) wide to finish the sides
- Overlocker
- Paint as required for the design
- Brushes

1 Measure the table and cut the netting to the same size as the top of the table. If it is not being made for a specific table, measurements of 82 x 130 cm (32¼ x 51 in) are generally used for the netting section.

2 Cut the 14 cm (5½ in) wide strips of fabric to the same length as the short sides of the netting.

3 Cut the 14 cm (5½ in) wide strips of fabric to about 28 cm (11 in) longer than the long sides of the netting.

4 Using an overlocker, finish the edges of the netting and strips of fabric.

5 Place the inside edges of the short strips on those of the netting, right sides together. Stitch 1 cm (⅜ in) wide seams. Iron the seams flat, placing the seam allowances under the side strip. Be careful that you don't burn the netting when you are ironing. Topstitch about 2 mm (1⁄16 in) from the fold on top of the side seam.

6 Repeat step 5 for the long sides of the tea shower.

7 Finish the tea shower with a 1 cm (⅜ in) wide hem.

8 Trace the design onto the borders. Trace one complete design with its centre at the exact centre of the short strips, and two designs with their centres at the quarter and three-quarter points of the long strips. You can also paint single motifs in the corners.

9 Paint the motifs and allow them to dry completely.

10 Fix the paint by pressing very well with an iron (see page 29). Be careful not to burn the net with the iron.

TO ADD A PERSONAL TOUCH TO YOUR GIFTS, MAKE YOUR OWN WRITING PAPER AND CARDS. USE THE SAME DESIGNS AS ON THE FABRIC, BUT MAKE THEM SMALLER AND SIMPLER. DRAW THE OUTLINES WITH DIFFERENT COLOURS OF INK AND COLOUR THEM IN WITH WATER PAINTS, FELT PENS OR EVEN CRAYONS.

TEA TOWELS

Turn a ready-made tea towel into something special by painting vegetables, fruit or flowers on it, or by appliqueing a painted motif. Tea towels are very useful gifts, and no one can have too many of them. A set of tea towels with an apron and pot holders are a marvellous gift for a kitchen tea.

Requirements
- Any bought tea towel, preferably of good quality
- Paint as required for the design
- Brushes
- Overlocker

1 Using a black pen, trace the design in one corner or along one side or on both short sides of the tea towel or onto a remnant of fabric.

2 Paint the design and allow it to dry completely.

3 Fix the paint using one of the heat treatments described on page 29.

4 If you have painted on a separate piece of fabric, overlock it all around with a 4 mm (³⁄₁₆ in) wide satin stitch that looks almost like a buttonhole finish. First test the stitching on another scrap of fabric.

5 Then stitch on the motif, using straight stitching and then zig-zag stitching all around.

POT HOLDERS

What cook would not be delighted to get a new set of pot holders? Make a good few sets at a time and keep them for those occasions when you need an unexpected gift.

Requirements
- 30 x 60 cm (12 x 24 in) strong cotton fabric for each pot holder
- 30 x 30 cm (12 x 12 in) thick wadding for each pot holder
- Paint as required for the design
- Brushes
- Thread for quilting
- Ribbon or painted fabric for a little loop

1 Cut the fabric into two pieces, each measuring 30 x 30 cm (12 x 12 in).

2 Using a black pen, trace the outlines of the design onto the fabric. Draw the outline of the design on the right side of both pieces of fabric so that they are mirror images of each other.

3 Paint the design on the front of the pot holder and then on the back of the pot holder. Remember to paint about 1 cm (³⁄₈ in) over the outlines so that there is no white line to be seen when the back and front are stitched together.

4 If you are going to have a coloured loop, paint an extra bit of fabric in a plain shade.

5 Allow the paint to dry completely before you move on to the next step.

6 Fix the paint using one of the heat treatments described on page 29.

7 Neatly cut out the front of the pot holder, including its seam allowance. Pin the front of the pot holder to the wadding. If you are only going to quilt the top of the pot holder, do it now (see page 90).

8 Stitch along the outline of the pot holder, through the wadding and front, to serve as a guideline when you are stitching the front and back together.

9 Cut the wadding to the same size as the pot holder plus seam allowance.

10 Make the loop by cutting a 4 x 16 cm (1⅝ x 6¼ in) strip for each loop. Fold the fabric in half lengthwise and then fold the raw edges to the inside as far as possible. Topstitch the sides close to the edge. Decide where the loop is to be placed on the pot holder. Fold the loop in half and pin it to the top of the front of the pot holder, with the raw edges of the loop on the raw edge of the pot holder.

11 Pin the back and front of the pot holder together, right sides facing.

12 Stitch over the stitching done in step 8 with the wadding facing up. Start and finish by working back and forth. Leave an opening of about 8 cm in the longest side for turning the pot holder right way out.

13 Snip notches around the curves of the seam so that it forms a smooth curve when turned inside out.

14 Turn the pot holder right way out and smooth out the seams with your fingers. Sew up the opening with invisible overhand stitches.

15 Iron the pot holder carefully and thoroughly.

16 If the quilting on the back is meant to be seen, this is the time to do it. If the pot holder is not quilted at all, topstitch about 2 mm (1/16 in) from the edge to ensure that the pot holder is nice and firm.

MAKE YOUR OWN GIFT WRAP TO MATCH YOUR PAINTED GIFTS BY DRAWING THE SAME MOTIFS ON BROWN PAPER OR ON ORDINARY WHITE, CLEAN NEWSPRINT. THE OUTLINES OF THE MOTIFS CAN BE DRAWN WITH COLOURED PENS OR THE MOTIFS CAN BE COLOURED IN WITH FELT PENS. FABRIC PAINT WOULD NOT BE SUITABLE FOR THIN PAPER LIKE THIS AS IT MAKES THE PAPER TOO WET.

Pot holders, hand towels, tea towels and tea showers are just a few of the articles that can be made from painted fabric.

APRONS

Any of the designs in this book will look good on an apron, and vegetables are particularly suitable. An apron makes a wonderful gift for a man who enjoys cooking and braaiing.

Requirements

- 1 x 0.75 m (39 x 30 in) unbleached linen
- 2 m (79 in) white tape, 2 cm (¾ in) wide, for the neck strip and waist fastenings
- Paint as required for the design
- Brushes

1 Prepare the fabric for the apron by washing it and ironing it thoroughly.

2 Draw the apron pattern on a piece of paper according to the diagram on page 127. The pattern allows for a 1.5 cm (⅝ in) hem all round.

3 Cut out the apron according to the pattern.

4 Using a black pen, trace the outlines of the design onto the fabric.

5 Paint the design and allow it to dry completely.

6 Fix the paint using one of the heat treatments described on page 29.

7 Make a double hem by folding over 0.5 cm (³⁄₁₆ in) and then 1 cm (⅜ in). Stitch right round the apron, 1 cm (⅜ in) from the edge.

Use a single design on an apron to keep it simple and uncluttered.

8 Measure the length of the tape that goes around the neck and stitch it neatly and securely in place. An average length is approximately 56 cm (22 in), but make sure that it passes easily over the head.

9 Firmly attach the two tapes that go around the waist. Make these tapes 70 cm (28 in) long. Press the raw edges of the tapes onto a hot plate on the stove to seal them and ensure that they do not fray. If the tapes are made of pure cotton, however, you'll have to sew a little hem, since heat will not seal cotton.

SHOPPING BAGS

Requirements

- 2 pieces of fabric, each about 40 x 50 cm (16 x 20 in), for the bag
- 2 pieces of fabric, each about 8 x 80 cm (3¼ x 31 in), for the handles
- Paint as required for the design
- Brushes
- Overlocker

1 Cut the fabric into neat rectangles before you start painting. The measurements of the finished bag are about 34 x 42 cm (13½ x 16½ in). Mark the painting area with a purple marking pen, allowing about 3 cm (1¼ in) for seams on the sides and about 5 cm (2 in) for a hem at the top. If you don't mark off these areas, part of the design may disappear into the seams or hem.

2 Using a black pen, trace the outlines of the design onto the fabric.

3 Paint the design on the fabric and leave it to dry completely.

4 Fix the paint using one of the heat treatments described on page 29.

5 Stitch up the sides and bottom of the bag. Cut the seams about 1 cm (⅜ in) wide and overlock them. Turn the bag inside out and neatly iron the seams flat.

6 Fold the strips of fabric for the handles in half lengthwise and stitch them up using a 1 cm (⅜ in) seam. Turn them

Bags like these are particularly popular among students as satchels for books.

inside out and iron them neatly along the seam. Topstitch two rows approximately 2 mm (1/16 in) from the edges so that the handles stay flat and firm. Overlock the two ends of the handles.

7 Overlock the top edge of the bag and fold the seam 4 cm (1⅝ in) to the inside. Stitch the hem with double stitching.

8 Pin the handles to the inside of the bag, 5.5 cm (2¼ in) from the side seams and with their edges parallel to the upper row of stitching of the top seam. Stitch the handles securely to the bag.

ROMAN BLINDS

The secret to this kind of blind is neat and accurate work and good, strong fabric. The more careful you are at the start, the better the result. Two heads are also better than one and if there's someone who can help measure, hold, saw and drill, it's all much easier.

Requirements

- Fabric with the design already painted true on the fabric. Use strong fabric which is preferably woven square. The fabric must be at least 5 cm (2 in) bigger all round than the completed blind.
- Fabric for the lining – firm fabric with a thread that pulls easily works best
- Purple marking pen
- Long, strong ruler
- Velcro
- Flat aluminium strip or wooden slat to use as a weight at the bottom – 1 cm (⅜ in) shorter than the completed width of the blind
- Dowels with a diameter of 8–10 mm (⅓ in), 1 cm (⅜ in) shorter than the width of the blind
- Plastic rings
- 20 x 10 mm (¾ x ⅜ in) wooden slat for attaching to the wall
- Fabric to cover wooden slat
- Stapling gun and staples
- Screw eyes
- Cord
- Knot cover
- Screws with wall plugs
- Cleat with screws

1 Measure the size of the window recess and draw it out on a piece of paper.

2 Determine the completed length and width of the blind as follows and draw in the measurements on the sketch (see page 127 for an example): If the blind is to fit within the window recess, deduct 1 cm (⅜ in) from the length and width so that the blind can move with ease. Make quite sure that the window itself is precisely square and true otherwise the blind will not fit when it is finished. If it is not quite square, make the necessary adjustments so that the blind will fit. If the blind is to hang over the window recess, add approximately 5 cm (2 in) to each side and about 10 cm (4 in) to the top and bottom.

3 Now calculate the spacing of the tucks for the dowels and draw them on the diagram. Then mark all these measurements on the lining of the blind. Calculate the spacing of the stitching on the blind as follows:
- Draw the line for the first stitching 30–33 cm (12–13 in) from the top;
- Allow 25–27 cm (9¾–10¾ in) for each following section;
- The remaining part forms the flap that includes the hem.

4 Calculate the spacing of the tucks on the lining and also indicate it on the sketch:
- Draw the line for the first tuck 1 cm (⅜ in) farther from the top than that of the blind – the lining is 0.5 cm (³⁄₁₆ in) shorter than the blind and 1.5 cm (⅝ in) is added for each side of the tuck for the first dowel. Leave 3 cm (1¼ in) more for each section than for the blind, to make provision for the tucks through which the dowels are going to be slotted;
- The bottom part can be 0.5 cm (³⁄₁₆ in) shorter than the blind so that the lining lies flat under the hem.

5 To allow for the hems, add the following to the final measurements: approximately 4.5 cm (1¾ in) on both sides, 3 cm (1¼ in) at the top and 10 cm (4 in) at the bottom. Cut out the fabric for the blind.

6 Cut the fabric for the lining 2 cm (¾ in) narrower than the blind. If you use good sateen fabric, you can use a marker to indicate the outlines of the lining, the fold marks of the hems and tucks for the dowels and pull the threads. It might look like a lot of extra work, but in the end it saves a great deal of pulling and pushing.

7 Iron the side seams of the lining along the marks of the pulled thread.

8 With the hems to the inside, iron a fold on the centremost mark of the three pulled threads for each dowel and pin the other two marks precisely on top of each other. Take note: no side seams are stitched by machine, they are only ironed in.

9 Stitch precisely on the two marks that have been pinned, so forming the first tuck. It is very important that you work accurately at this stage, otherwise the dowels might not slide through the slots.

10 Repeat steps 8 and 9 for each tuck.

11 Using the marking pen, mark the side seams of the blind very clearly or tack a clear mark where the fold is to go, as well as all the positions of all the stitchings for the tucks for the dowels.

12 Iron in the side seams very carefully.

13 Place the blind fabric flat on a table with its right side facing down. Place the lining with its right side up on the blind fabric, so that the tucks for the dowels are facing upwards.

14 Place the centremost tuck on the mark on the blind, exactly 1 cm (⅜ in) from the folds of the side seams of the blind. The result is better if you start at the middle tuck and not from the top to the bottom. Pin the lining to the blind very accurately and carefully and then stitch to the blind. Use a fairly large machine stitch and strengthen the ends of the tuck by working back and forth a few times. However, work very carefully and accurately since the bottom is the front of the blind and therefore visible. Roll up the part of the lining and blind that has to go under the machine on the right from the outside to the inside before you start working – if it is forced or pushed through in a bundle, the fabric will pull and will become misshapen.

15 Repeat step 14 for each tuck. Each time smooth out the two pieces of fabric with your hands and then pin together very carefully. After each stitching, test whether the blind hangs free and doesn't make any bags. Should this happen, you'll have to pull it out and try again.

16 Iron in a hem of 3 cm (1¼ in) at the top of the blind and fold the top piece of lining neatly under the hem. If the lining rolls over at the top, cut it about 0.5 cm (³⁄₁₆ in) shorter. Stitch down 1 cm (⅜ in) from the top.

17 Stitch the top side of the velcro with the top edge on the stitching of step 16 to the inside of the blind. First stitch the velcro at the top and then at the bottom in the same direction so that it does not pull skew. There are thus three stitchings visible on the front – two are approximately 1 mm (¹⁄₁₆ in) apart at the top and one is approximately 1.5 cm (⅝ in) below these stitchings.

18 Iron a turn-up of 2 cm (¾ in) and then an 8 cm (3¼ in) hem at the bottom of the blind and fold in the bottom edge of the lining. Stitch through the lining and the blind fabric and leave the sides of the hem open.

19 Slide the flat aluminium strip or wooden slat through the hem at the bottom and sew up the openings in the sides with slipstitches.

20 Slip the dowels into the openings in the tucks. Sew up the openings of the tucks with slipstitches.

21 Lay the blind flat with the lining facing upwards. Measure and mark the positions of the rings on the tucks. The first and last vertical lines of rings are placed approximately 3 cm (1¼ in) from the sides of the blind. The rest of the vertical lines ought to be spaced evenly about 30 cm (12 in) apart over the width of the blind. Sew all the rings firmly in position on the folds of the tucks.

22 Saw the top strip of wood to the same length as the completed width of the blind. Cover it neatly with fabric and staple the rough side of the velcro to the front of the wooden slat.

23 Drill holes through the slat for screwing it onto the wall.

24 Screw in the screw eyes to the underside of the slat so that their positions coincide with that of the vertical row of rings on the blind. Screw in an extra eye on the side where the drawstrings are going to be threaded through together.

25 Press the soft velcro to the rough velcro to attach the blind to the slat.

26 Knot the cord firmly to the lowest ring of the first vertical row. Thread it through the other rings, through the screw eyes in the slat and to the side of the blind where the drawstrings are kept together. Repeat with the rest of the vertical rows of rings.

27 Pull all the cords in at the same time so that the blind pulls up evenly. Make sure that the folds hang evenly.

28 Hold the drawstrings tightly and allow the blind to drop to the bottom. Loosely knot the cords together about 50 cm (20 in) from the upper slat.

29 Loosen the cords again and thread them up to the top ring in every row. Loosen the velcro and put the blind aside.

30 Screw the slat to the wall or window-frame through the holes and thread the cords through again. Carefully attach the velcro again in the proper position and thread the ends of the cords through the screw eyes at the bottom of the slat.

31 Now knot the ends of the cords tightly and attach a knot cover to the ends of the cords. Lightly singe all the ends of the cords to prevent them from fraying.

32 Screw a cleat to the wall or window-frame on the same side as the drawstrings so that the cord can be wound around it when the blind is pulled up.

The secret to a successful blind is neat and accurate work and strong, good quality fabric.

BOX FRAMES

This is a very cheap and effective method of framing articles. When a couple of these frames are hung together, the effect can be very striking.

Requirements

- Use strong fabric which is preferably woven true. The fabric must be at least 10 cm (4 in) larger than the completed frame. The measurements of these examples are 70 x 70 cm (28 x 28 in). The size of the fabric is thus 75 x 75 cm (29½ x 29½ in) to make provision for the fabric being pulled over the edges and stapled to the back.
- Square-cut wood 2.5 x 2.5 cm (1 x 1 in) or strong skirting-boards. Any wood which does not warp and is without cracks, like good-quality pine or meranti, can be used. The measurements will also depend on the eventual size of the frame. You'll need thicker wood for a large artwork.
- Staple gun and staples
- Joiner's glue
- Nails

1 Make sure that the corners are square – remember, a skew piece of fabric can't be pulled straight later on. If you work correctly from the start, you'll save yourself a lot of bother in the long run.

2 Using a pencil, draw a guideline on the wrong side of the fabric. This line is drawn at a distance that is twice the width of the frame, from the outer edge of the fabric. Carefully iron folds into the fabric along these lines. These folds will then serve as guidelines for the outlines of the finished article. Trace the design onto the fabric and then paint it. Leave the paint to dry completely.

3 Iron the fabric very well on the wrong side to fix the paint.

4 Each side of the frame is the width of the wood shorter than the finished length of the side. In other words, where the sides measure 70 cm (28 in) and the wood is 2.5 cm (1 in) wide, each piece of wood is therefore 67.5 cm (26½ in) long. Stick the wood together with joiner's glue and then attach the two pieces of wood on each corner with two nails as well. Allow the glue to dry completely.

5 Take care that the ironed folds, which should still be slightly visible, lie on the outer edge of the frame. Firmly staple the first side of the fabric to the back, but leave the last 5 cm (2 in) of the sides loose so that you can make neat folds at each corner.

6 Staple the next side and keep on until all four sides are stapled to the back of the frame.

7 Fold the corners flat and staple down.

Box frames are an easy and
inexpensive way to frame your works of art.

DESIGNS & DIAGRAMS

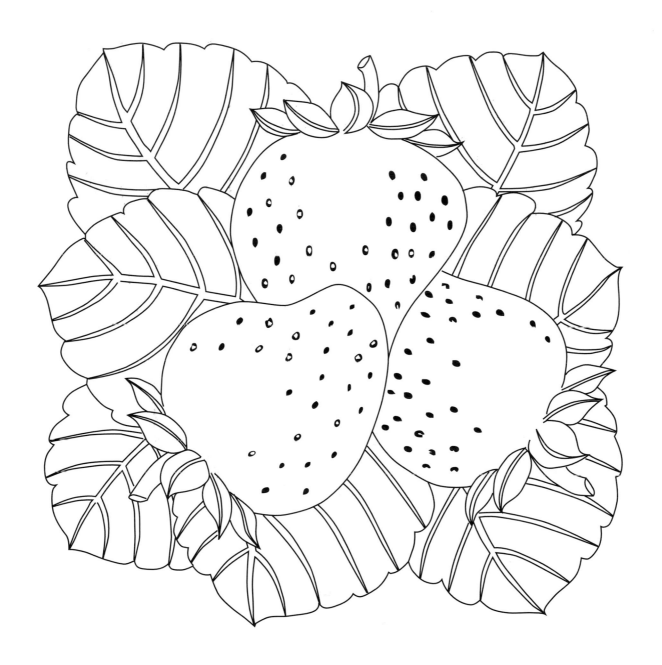

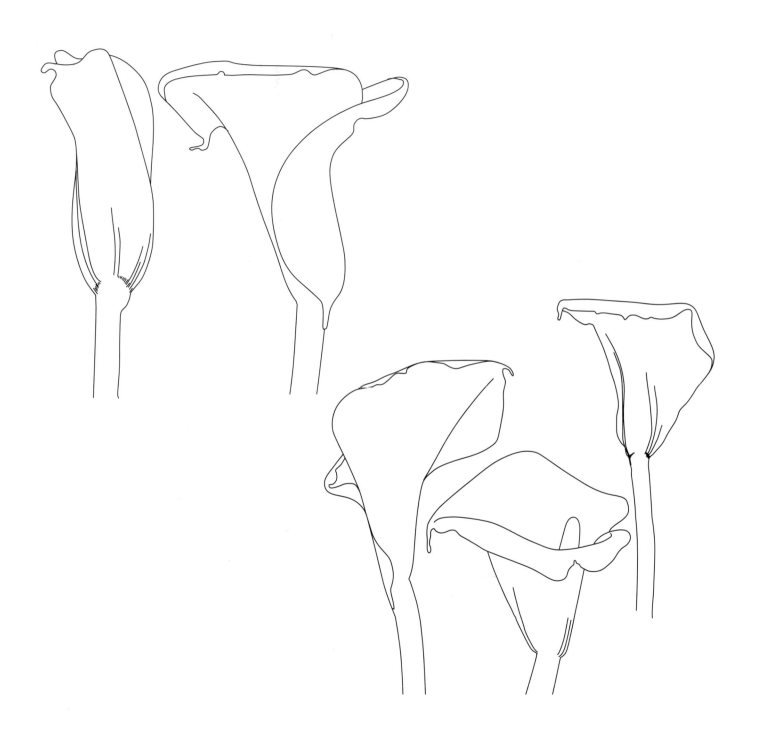

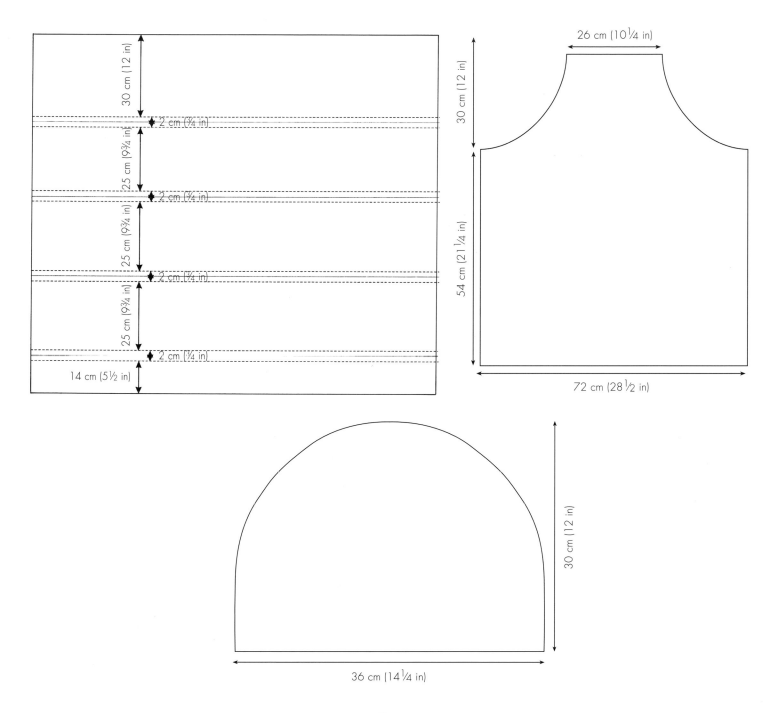

30 cm (12 in)

2 cm (¾ in)

25 cm (9¾ in)

2 cm (¾ in)

25 cm (9¾ in)

2 cm (¾ in)

25 cm (9¾ in)

2 cm (¾ in)

14 cm (5½ in)

26 cm (10¼ in)

30 cm (12 in)

54 cm (21¼ in)

72 cm (28½ in)

30 cm (12 in)

36 cm (14¼ in)

INDEX

(Numbers in *italics* refer to illustrations, numbers in **bold** refer to photographs)